Bangladeshi Cookbook
Authentic Recipes

UNCOVER THE RICH AND DIVERSE FLAVORS OF BANGLADESH

SHARMIN L. AKTER

AUTHENTIC BANGLADESHI COOKBOOK RECIPES
Uncover the Rich and Diverse Flavors of Bangladesh.

© Sharmin L. Akter
© E.G.P. Editorial

Printed in USA.
ISBN-13: 9798390966273

Copyright © All rights reserved.

"Authentic Bangladeshi Cookbook Recipes" is a comprehensive guide to the rich and flavorful cuisine of Bangladesh.

This cookbook provides step-by-step instructions for preparing a variety of traditional Bangladeshi dishes, showcasing the diverse range of flavors that make up this unique culinary landscape.

Each recipe includes a full list of ingredients and clear instructions, making it easy for home cooks to recreate the authentic flavors of Bangladesh in their own kitchens.

Whether you are a seasoned cook or a beginner, this cookbook is the perfect starting point for anyone looking to explore the traditional dishes of this fascinating and delicious cuisine.

Let's discover the wonders of Bangladeshi cuisine!

TABLE OF CONTENTS

BREAKFAST 5
APPETIZERS & SNACKS 13
RICE DISHES 31
CURRIES AND STEWS 43
FISH & SEAFOOD 75
MEATS 91
BREADS 99
BEVERAGES 111
PICKLES & CHUTNEYS 117
SALADS 125
SOUPS 128
SIDES 136
STREET FOOD 141
DESSERTS & SWEETS 148
RECIPES LIST 166

BREAKFAST

CHIRE BHAJA (FRIED FLATTENED RICE)

Ingredients:

- 3 cups flattened rice (poha)
- 1 onion, chopped
- 1 green chili, chopped
- 1 tsp salt
- 1 tsp sugar
- 1 tsp red chili powder
- 1 tsp cumin powder
- 1 tsp coriander powder
- 1 tbsp lemon juice
- Vegetable oil for frying

Instructions:

1. Rinse the flattened rice in a fine mesh strainer under running water until softened, about 2-3 minutes.

2. In a large mixing bowl, mix together the softened flattened rice, chopped onion, chopped green chili, salt, sugar, red chili powder, cumin powder, coriander powder, and lemon juice.

3. Heat the vegetable oil in a large frying pan over medium heat.

4. Take a handful of the flattened rice mixture and shape into small patties.

5. Fry the patties in the hot oil until golden brown, about 2-3 minutes on each side.

6. Remove the fried patties and set aside to drain on paper towels to remove excess oil.

7. Repeat the process with the remaining flattened rice mixture until all the patties have been fried.

8. Serve the chire bhaja immediately, garnished with additional chopped cilantro and a squeeze of lemon juice, if desired.

RADHABALLABHI (STUFFED DEEP-FRIED BREAD)

Ingredients:

- **For the dough:**
    - 2 cups all-purpose flour
    - 1 tsp salt
    - 1 tsp sugar
    - 1 tbsp vegetable oil
    - Water, as needed

- **For the stuffing:**
    - 1 cup boiled and mashed potatoes
    - 1/2 cup paneer, crumbled
    - 1 small onion, chopped
    - 2 tbsp chopped cilantro
    - 1 tsp red chili powder
    - 1 tsp chaat masala
    - 1 tsp roasted cumin powder
    - 1 tsp salt

- Vegetable oil for deep-frying

Instructions:

1. To make the dough, mix together the all-purpose flour, salt, sugar, vegetable oil, and water in a large mixing bowl until a soft dough forms.

2. Cover the dough and let rest for 15-20 minutes.

3. To make the stuffing, mix together the boiled and mashed potatoes, crumbled paneer, chopped onion, chopped cilantro, red chili powder, chaat masala, roasted cumin powder, and salt in a large mixing bowl until well combined.

4. Divide the dough into small balls and roll each ball into a thin circle.

5. Place a spoonful of the stuffing mixture in the center of each dough circle.

6. Fold the edges of the dough circle up and around the stuffing mixture, pinch the edges to seal, and form into a ball shape.

7. Heat the vegetable oil for deep-frying in a large pot over medium heat.

8. Fry the stuffed dough balls in the hot oil until golden brown, about 2-3 minutes on each side.

9. Remove the fried dough balls and set aside to drain on paper towels to remove excess oil.

10. Serve the radhaballabhi immediately, garnished with additional chopped cilantro and a squeeze of lemon juice, if desired.

MUGHLAI PARATHA
(STUFFED AND FRIED BREAD)

Ingredients:

- **For the dough:**

    - 2 cups all-purpose flour
    - 1 tsp salt
    - 1 tsp sugar
    - 1 tbsp vegetable oil
    - Water, as needed

- **For the stuffing:**

    - 1 cup boiled and mashed potatoes
    - 1/2 cup paneer, crumbled
    - 1 small onion, chopped
    - 2 tbsp chopped cilantro
    - 1 tsp red chili powder
    - 1 tsp chaat masala
    - 1 tsp roasted cumin powder
    - 1 tsp salt

- Vegetable oil for shallow-frying

Instructions:

1. To make the dough, mix together the all-purpose flour, salt, sugar, vegetable oil, and water in a large mixing bowl until a soft dough forms.

2. Cover the dough and let rest for 15-20 minutes.

3. To make the stuffing, mix together the boiled and mashed potatoes, crumbled paneer, chopped onion, chopped cilantro, red chili powder, chaat masala, roasted cumin powder, and salt in a large mixing bowl until well combined.

4. Divide the dough into small balls and roll each ball into a thin circle.

5. Place a spoonful of the stuffing mixture in the center of each dough circle.

6. Fold the edges of the dough circle up and around the stuffing mixture, pinch the edges to seal, and form into a ball shape.

7. Heat the vegetable oil for shallow-frying in a large frying pan over medium heat.

8. Place the stuffed dough balls in the hot oil and cook until the bottom is golden brown, about 2-3 minutes.

9. Flip the paratha over and cook until the other side is golden brown, about 2-3 minutes.

10. Remove the paratha and set aside to drain on paper towels to remove excess oil.

11. Repeat the process with the remaining stuffed dough balls until all the paratha have been cooked.

12. Serve the mughlai paratha immediately, garnished with additional chopped cilantro and a squeeze of lemon juice, if desired.

ALUR DOM (SPICY POTATO CURRY)

Ingredients:

- 3 medium potatoes, peeled and chopped
- 1 small onion, chopped
- 2 cloves garlic, minced
- 1 inch ginger, grated

- 2 medium tomatoes, chopped
- 1 tsp cumin seeds
- 1 tsp coriander powder
- 1 tsp turmeric powder
- 1 tsp red chili powder
- 1 tsp garam masala
- 1 tsp salt
- 2 tbsp vegetable oil
- 1 cup water
- 2 tbsp chopped cilantro, for garnish

Instructions:

1. Heat the vegetable oil in a large saucepan over medium heat.

2. Add the cumin seeds and cook until fragrant, about 1 minute.

3. Add the chopped onion, minced garlic, and grated ginger and cook until the onion is soft and translucent, about 5 minutes.

4. Add the chopped tomatoes, coriander powder, turmeric powder, red chili powder, garam masala, and salt to the saucepan and cook until the tomatoes are soft and have broken down, about 5 minutes.

5. Add the chopped potatoes and water to the saucepan and bring to a boil.

6. Reduce the heat to low, cover the saucepan, and simmer until the potatoes are tender, about 10-15 minutes.

7. Remove the saucepan from heat and let the alur dom cool slightly.

8. Serve the alur dom hot, garnished with chopped cilantro, if desired.

DIMER JHOL (EGG CURRY)

Ingredients:

- 6 large eggs
- 1 small onion, chopped
- 2 cloves garlic, minced
- 1 inch ginger, grated
- 2 medium tomatoes, chopped
- 1 tsp cumin seeds
- 1 tsp coriander powder
- 1 tsp turmeric powder
- 1 tsp red chili powder
- 1 tsp garam masala
- 1 tsp salt
- 2 tbsp vegetable oil
- 1 cup water
- 2 tbsp chopped cilantro, for garnish

Instructions:

1. Boil the eggs in a large saucepan of water until hard-boiled, about 10 minutes.

2. Peel the eggs and set aside.

3. Heat the vegetable oil in a large saucepan over medium heat.

4. Add the cumin seeds and cook until fragrant, about 1 minute.

5. Add the chopped onion, minced garlic, and grated ginger and cook until the onion is soft and translucent, about 5 minutes.

6. Add the chopped tomatoes, coriander powder, turmeric powder, red chili powder, garam masala, and salt to the saucepan and cook until the tomatoes are soft and have broken down, about 5 minutes.

7. Add the water to the saucepan and bring to a boil.

8. Cut the hard-boiled eggs into halves and add them to the saucepan.

9. Reduce the heat to low and let the egg curry simmer for about 5 minutes, until the sauce has thickened slightly.

10. Serve the dimer jhol hot, garnished with chopped cilantro, if desired.

APPETIZERS & SNACKS

SINGARA (SAMOSA)

Ingredients:

- 1 cup all-purpose flour
- 1/2 teaspoon salt
- 1/2 teaspoon ajwain seeds
- 2 tablespoons oil
- 1/2 cup water
- 1 cup boiled and mashed potatoes
- 1/2 teaspoon red chili powder
- 1/2 teaspoon coriander powder
- 1/2 teaspoon cumin powder
- 1/2 teaspoon mango powder
- 1/2 teaspoon garam masala
- 2 tablespoons chopped cilantro
- Oil for frying

Instructions:

1. In a large bowl, combine the flour, salt, ajwain seeds, and oil. Mix until the mixture resembles coarse crumbs.

2. Add water slowly, mixing until the dough comes together. Knead the dough for a few minutes until smooth.

3. In a separate bowl, mix together the mashed potatoes, red chili powder, coriander powder, cumin powder, mango powder, garam masala, and chopped cilantro. Divide the mixture into 12 equal parts.

4. Roll out the dough into a thin circle, cut the circle into two equal halves. Take one half, and form a cone by bringing one end to the other and sealing it with a little water. Fill the cone with one of the potato mixture balls, and seal the top of the cone.

5. Repeat with the rest of the dough and potato mixture.

6. Heat the oil in a large pan over medium heat. Fry the samosas until golden brown, about 3-4 minutes on each side.

7. Serve hot with chutney or sauce of your choice.

PIYAJU (LENTIL FRITTERS)

Ingredients:

- 1 cup yellow split lentils
- 1/2 teaspoon salt
- 1/2 teaspoon turmeric powder
- 1/2 teaspoon red chili powder
- 1/2 teaspoon cumin powder
- 1/2 teaspoon coriander powder
- 1/2 teaspoon baking powder
- 1/2 teaspoon sugar
- 1/2 teaspoon mango powder
- 1/2 teaspoon garam masala
- 2 tablespoons chopped cilantro
- Oil for frying

Instructions:

1. Rinse the yellow split lentils and soak in water for 30 minutes.

2. Drain the lentils and grind them into a smooth paste using a food processor or grinder.

3. In a large bowl, mix together the lentil paste, salt, turmeric powder, red chili powder, cumin powder, coriander powder, baking powder, sugar, mango powder, garam masala, and chopped cilantro.

4. Heat the oil in a large pan over medium heat. Using a spoon, drop spoonfuls of the lentil mixture into the hot oil. Fry until golden brown, about 2-3 minutes on each side.

5. Remove the fritters from the oil and drain on a paper towel-lined plate to remove any excess oil.

6. Serve hot with chutney or sauce of your choice.

BEGUNI (EGGPLANT FRITTERS)

Ingredients:

- 2 medium-sized eggplants
- 1 cup chickpea flour
- 1/2 teaspoon salt
- 1/2 teaspoon turmeric powder
- 1/2 teaspoon red chili powder
- 1/2 teaspoon cumin powder
- 1/2 teaspoon coriander powder
- 1/2 teaspoon baking powder
- 1/2 teaspoon sugar
- 1/2 teaspoon mango powder
- 1/2 teaspoon garam masala
- 2 tablespoons chopped cilantro
- Oil for frying

Instructions:

1. Slice the eggplants into 1/4 inch rounds.

2. In a large bowl, mix together the chickpea flour, salt, turmeric powder, red chili powder, cumin powder, coriander powder, baking powder, sugar, mango powder, garam masala, and chopped cilantro.

3. Heat the oil in a large pan over medium heat. Dip each eggplant slice into the chickpea flour mixture, coating both sides well. Fry until golden brown, about 2-3 minutes on each side.

4. Remove the fritters from the oil and drain on a paper towel-lined plate to remove any excess oil.

5. Serve hot with chutney or sauce of your choice.

ALOO CHOP (POTATO FRITTERS)

Ingredients:

- 2 medium-sized potatoes
- 1 cup all-purpose flour
- 1/2 teaspoon salt
- 1/2 teaspoon turmeric powder
- 1/2 teaspoon red chili powder
- 1/2 teaspoon cumin powder
- 1/2 teaspoon coriander powder
- 1/2 teaspoon baking powder
- 1/2 teaspoon sugar
-
- 1/2 teaspoon garam masala
- 2 tablespoons chopped cilantro
- Oil for frying

Instructions:

1. Boil or bake the potatoes until they are tender. Mash the potatoes and set aside to cool.

2. In a large bowl, mix together the flour, salt, turmeric powder, red chili powder, cumin powder, coriander powder, baking powder, sugar, mango powder, garam masala, and chopped cilantro.

3. Mix the mashed potatoes into the flour mixture until well combined.

4. Heat the oil in a large pan over medium heat. Using a spoon or your hands, form small balls out of the potato mixture and drop into the hot oil. Fry until golden brown, about 2-3 minutes on each side.

5. Remove the fritters from the oil and drain on a paper towel-lined plate to remove any excess oil.

6. Serve hot with chutney or sauce of your choice.

CHINGRI PAKORA (SHRIMP FRITTERS)

Ingredients:

- 1 pound large shrimp, peeled and deveined
- 1 cup all-purpose flour
- 1/2 teaspoon salt
- 1/2 teaspoon turmeric powder
- 1/2 teaspoon red chili powder
- 1/2 teaspoon cumin powder
- 1/2 teaspoon coriander powder
- 1/2 teaspoon baking powder
- 1/2 teaspoon sugar
- 1/2 teaspoon mango powder
- 1/2 teaspoon garam masala
- 2 tablespoons chopped cilantro
- Oil for frying

Instructions:

1. In a large bowl, mix together the flour, salt, turmeric powder, red chili powder, cumin powder, coriander powder, baking powder, sugar, mango powder, garam masala, and chopped cilantro.

2. Dip each shrimp into the flour mixture, coating well. Shake off any excess flour mixture.

3. Heat the oil in a large pan over medium heat. Fry the shrimp until golden brown, about 2-3 minutes on each side.

4. Remove the fritters from the oil and drain on a paper towel-lined plate to remove any excess oil.

5. Serve hot with chutney or sauce of your choice.

DALER BORA (LENTIL DUMPLINGS)

Ingredients:

- 1 cup yellow split lentils
- 1/2 teaspoon salt
- 1/2 teaspoon turmeric powder
- 1/2 teaspoon red chili powder
- 1/2 teaspoon cumin powder
- 1/2 teaspoon coriander powder
- 1/2 teaspoon baking powder
- 1/2 teaspoon sugar
- 1/2 teaspoon mango powder
- 1/2 teaspoon garam masala
- 2 tablespoons chopped cilantro
- Oil for frying

Instructions:

1. Rinse the yellow split lentils and soak in water for 30 minutes.

2. Drain the lentils and grind them into a smooth paste using a food processor or grinder.

3. In a large bowl, mix together the lentil paste, salt, turmeric powder, red chili powder, cumin powder, coriander powder, baking powder, sugar, mango powder, garam masala, and chopped cilantro.

4. Shape the mixture into small balls, about 1 inch in diameter.

5. Heat the oil in a large pan over medium heat. Fry the lentil balls until golden brown, about 2-3 minutes on each side.

6. Remove the dumplings from the oil and drain on a paper towel-lined plate to remove any excess oil.

7. Serve hot with chutney or sauce of your choice.

MURI GHONTO (PUFFED RICE SNACK)

Ingredients:

- 2 cups puffed rice
- 1 medium-sized potato, boiled and mashed
- 1/2 teaspoon salt
- 1/2 teaspoon turmeric powder
- 1/2 teaspoon red chili powder
- 1/2 teaspoon cumin powder
- 1/2 teaspoon coriander powder
- 1/2 teaspoon mango powder
- 1/2 teaspoon garam masala
- 2 tablespoons chopped cilantro

Instructions:

1. In a large bowl, mix together the puffed rice, mashed potato, salt, turmeric powder, red chili powder, cumin powder, coriander powder, mango powder, garam masala, and chopped cilantro.

2. Mix everything together until the puffed rice is well coated with the spices and potato mixture.

3. Serve as a snack or with a side of chutney or sauce of your choice.

JHAL MURI (SPICY PUFFED RICE)

Ingredients:

- 2 cups puffed rice
- 2 tablespoons oil
- 1 teaspoon mustard seeds
- 1 teaspoon cumin seeds
- 1/2 teaspoon asafoetida (hing) powder
- 1/2 teaspoon salt
- 1/2 teaspoon turmeric powder
- 1/2 teaspoon red chili powder
- 1/2 teaspoon cumin powder
- 1/2 teaspoon coriander powder
- 1/2 teaspoon mango powder
- 1/2 teaspoon garam masala
- 2 tablespoons chopped cilantro

Instructions:

1. In a large bowl, mix together the puffed rice, salt, turmeric powder, red chili powder, cumin powder, coriander powder, mango powder, garam masala, and chopped cilantro.

2. Heat the oil in a large pan over medium heat. Add the mustard seeds and cumin seeds, and let them splutter for a few seconds.

3. Add the asafoetida powder and let it cook for a few seconds.

4. Add the puffed rice mixture to the pan and stir to combine with the spices and oil.

5. Serve as a snack or with a side of chutney or sauce of your choice.

CHOTPOTI (SPICY CHICKPEA SNACK)

Ingredients:

- 1 can chickpeas, drained and rinsed
- 2 tablespoons oil
- 1 teaspoon mustard seeds
- 1 teaspoon cumin seeds
- 1/2 teaspoon asafoetida (hing) powder
- 1/2 teaspoon salt
- 1/2 teaspoon turmeric powder
- 1/2 teaspoon red chili powder
- 1/2 teaspoon cumin powder
- 1/2 teaspoon coriander powder
- 1/2 teaspoon mango powder
- 1/2 teaspoon garam masala
- 2 tablespoons chopped cilantro

Instructions:

1. In a large bowl, mix together the chickpeas, salt, turmeric powder, red chili powder, cumin powder, coriander powder, mango powder, garam masala, and chopped cilantro.

2. Heat the oil in a large pan over medium heat. Add the mustard seeds and cumin seeds, and let them splutter for a few seconds.

3. Add the asafoetida powder and let it cook for a few seconds.

4. Add the chickpea mixture to the pan and stir to combine with the spices and oil.

5. Cook until the chickpeas are heated through and the spices are well combined, about 5-7 minutes.

6. Serve as a snack or with a side of chutney or sauce of your choice.

FUCHKA (PANIPURI)

Ingredients:

- 24 small round puri shells
- 2 cups water
- 1 teaspoon salt
- 1 teaspoon sugar
- 1/2 teaspoon black salt
- 1/2 teaspoon roasted cumin powder
- 1/2 teaspoon red chili powder
- 2 cups boiled and mashed potatoes
- 2 tablespoons tamarind chutney
- 2 tablespoons mint chutney
- 2 cups chickpeas, boiled and drained
- 1 cup finely chopped onions
- 2 tablespoons finely chopped cilantro

Instructions:

1. In a large bowl, mix together the water, salt, sugar, black salt, roasted cumin powder, and red chili powder to make the water filling.

2. In another bowl, mix together the mashed potatoes, tamarind chutney, mint chutney, chickpeas, chopped onions, and chopped cilantro to make the potato filling.

3. To assemble the fuchka, take one puri shell and make a small hole in the center using your finger or the back of a spoon.

4. Fill the puri shell with a small spoonful of the water filling and then a small spoonful of the potato filling.

5. Repeat the process with the remaining puri shells and fillings.

6. Serve the fuchka immediately and enjoy the crunchy, spicy, and tangy flavors in each bite!

VEGETABLE CUTLET

Ingredients:

- 1 cup boiled and mashed potatoes
- 1 cup mixed vegetables (such as carrots, green beans, peas, corn), boiled and chopped
- 1/2 teaspoon salt
- 1/2 teaspoon turmeric powder
- 1/2 teaspoon red chili powder
- 1/2 teaspoon cumin powder
- 1/2 teaspoon coriander powder
- 1/2 teaspoon mango powder
- 1/2 teaspoon garam masala
- 2 tablespoons chopped cilantro
- 1 cup breadcrumbs
- Oil for frying

Instructions:

1. In a large bowl, mix together the boiled and mashed potatoes, chopped mixed vegetables, salt, turmeric powder, red chili powder, cumin powder, coriander powder, mango powder, garam masala, and chopped cilantro.

2. Divide the mixture into equal portions and shape each portion into a flat patty or cutlet shape.

3. Place the breadcrumbs in a shallow dish and coat each cutlet with the breadcrumbs, pressing firmly so the breadcrumbs adhere to the cutlet.

4. Heat the oil in a large frying pan over medium heat. Once the oil is hot, add the cutlets to the pan and fry until golden brown on both sides, about 3-4 minutes per side.

5. Remove the cutlets from the pan and place on a paper towel-lined plate to drain any excess oil.

6. Serve hot with ketchup or chutney of your choice.

SHOBJI PITHA
(VEGETABLE STUFFED RICE CAKE)

Ingredients:

- 1 cup rice, soaked for 2 hours
- 1 cup mixed vegetables (such as carrots, green beans, peas, corn), chopped
- 1/2 teaspoon salt
- 1/2 teaspoon turmeric powder
- 1/2 teaspoon red chili powder
- 1/2 teaspoon cumin powder
- 1/2 teaspoon coriander powder
- 1/2 teaspoon mango powder
- 1/2 teaspoon garam masala
- 2 tablespoons chopped cilantro
- 2 tablespoons oil

Instructions:

1. In a large bowl, mix together the soaked rice, chopped mixed vegetables, salt, turmeric powder, red chili powder, cumin powder, coriander powder, mango powder, garam masala, and chopped cilantro.

2. Heat the oil in a large pan over medium heat. Add the rice and vegetable mixture to the pan and stir to combine with the spices and oil.

3. Cook the mixture, stirring occasionally, until the rice is fully cooked and the vegetables are tender, about 20-25 minutes.

4. Let the mixture cool slightly, then shape it into small cakes or patties.

5. Serve the shobji pitha hot with a side of chutney or sauce of your choice.

CHITAI PITHA (THIN RICE CAKE)

Ingredients:

- 1 cup rice flour
- 1 cup water
- 1/2 teaspoon salt
- 2 tablespoons ghee or oil

Instructions:

1. In a large bowl, mix together the rice flour, water, salt, and ghee or oil to form a smooth batter.

2. Heat a non-stick griddle or pan over medium heat. Pour a thin layer of the batter onto the griddle and spread it evenly using a spatula.

3. Cook the pitha until the bottom is lightly browned, about 2-3 minutes, then flip and cook the other side for an additional 2-3 minutes.

4. Repeat the process with the remaining batter to make more pithas.

5. Serve the chitai pitha hot with a side of chutney or sauce of your choice.

PATISHAPTA (SWEET RICE CREPES)

Ingredients:

- 1 cup rice flour
- 1/2 cup all-purpose flour
- 1 cup milk
- 1/2 cup sugar
- 1/2 teaspoon salt
- 1/2 teaspoon cardamom powder
- 1/2 cup grated coconut
- 2 tablespoons chopped nuts (such as almonds or pistachios), optional
- Oil or ghee for frying

Instructions:

1. In a large bowl, mix together the rice flour, all-purpose flour, milk, sugar, salt, cardamom powder, grated coconut, and chopped nuts (if using).

2. Heat a non-stick griddle or pan over medium heat and lightly grease with oil or ghee.

3. Pour a small amount of the batter onto the griddle and spread it into a thin, even layer using a spatula.

4. Cook the patishapta until the bottom is lightly browned, about 2-3 minutes, then flip and cook the other side for an additional 2-3 minutes.

5. Repeat the process with the remaining batter to make more patishaptas.

6. Serve the patishapta hot, drizzled with a little extra sugar or topped with more grated coconut and chopped nuts if desired.

BHAPA PITHA (STEAMED RICE CAKE)

Ingredients:

- 1 cup rice flour
- 1 cup water
- 1/2 teaspoon salt
- 1/2 teaspoon sugar
- 1/2 teaspoon cardamom powder
- 1/2 cup grated coconut
- 2 tablespoons chopped nuts (such as almonds or pistachios), optional

Instructions:

1. In a large bowl, mix together the rice flour, water, salt, sugar, cardamom powder, grated coconut, and chopped nuts (if using).

2. Pour the mixture into a greased heat-proof dish, such as a silicone steaming mold or a heat-proof bowl.

3. Place the dish in a steamer basket and steam over boiling water for 20-25 minutes, or until the pitha is fully cooked and firm to the touch.

4. Remove the bhapa pitha from the steamer and let it cool slightly before slicing and serving.

5. Serve the bhapa pitha hot with a side of chutney or sauce of your choice.

PULI PITHA (SWEET RICE DUMPLINGS)

Ingredients:

- 1 cup rice flour
- 1/2 cup all-purpose flour
- 1 cup water
- 1/2 cup sugar
- 1/2 teaspoon salt
- 1/2 teaspoon cardamom powder
- 1/2 cup grated coconut
- 2 tablespoons chopped nuts (such as almonds or pistachios), optional
- Water for boiling

Instructions:

1. In a large bowl, mix together the rice flour, all-purpose flour, water, sugar, salt, cardamom powder, grated coconut, and chopped nuts (if using).

2. Divide the mixture into equal portions and shape each portion into a small ball or dumpling.

3. Bring a large pot of water to a boil and gently add the dumplings to the boiling water.

4. Cook the dumplings until they float to the surface and are fully cooked, about 10-15 minutes.

5. Remove the dumplings from the pot and let them cool slightly before serving.

6. Serve the puli pitha hot with a side of chutney or sauce of your choice.

CHUI JHAL MURI (RICE PUFF SNACK)

Ingredients:

- 2 cups puffed rice
- 1/2 cup chopped vegetables (such as onion, tomato, cucumber, and carrot)
- 1/4 cup roasted peanuts
- 1/4 cup chopped cilantro
- 1 tablespoon lemon juice
- 1 teaspoon salt
- 1/2 teaspoon red chili powder
- 1/2 teaspoon cumin powder
- 1/2 teaspoon coriander powder
- 1/2 teaspoon mango powder

Instructions:

1. In a large bowl, mix together the puffed rice, chopped vegetables, roasted peanuts, chopped cilantro, lemon juice, salt, red chili powder, cumin powder, coriander powder, and mango powder.

2. Toss the mixture well to combine all the ingredients and spices evenly.

3. Serve the chui jhal muri immediately as a snack or light lunch.

JHURI BHAJA (THIN POTATO CRISPS)

Ingredients:

- 2 large potatoes
- Salt to taste
- 1/2 teaspoon red chili powder
- 1/2 teaspoon cumin powder

- 1/2 teaspoon coriander powder
- 1/2 teaspoon mango powder
- Oil for frying

Instructions:

1. Peel the potatoes and slice them very thinly, about 1/8 inch thickness.

2. In a large bowl, mix together the sliced potatoes, salt, red chili powder, cumin powder, coriander powder, and mango powder.

3. Heat the oil in a large frying pan over medium heat.

4. Once the oil is hot, add the seasoned potato slices to the pan in a single layer and fry until golden brown on both sides, about 3-4 minutes per side.

5. Remove the jhuri bhaja from the pan and place on a paper towel-lined plate to drain any excess oil.

6. Serve the jhuri bhaja hot as a snack or side dish.

RICE DISHES

BHUNA KHICHURI
(FRIED RICE AND LENTIL DISH)

Ingredients:

- 1 cup rice
- 1/2 cup lentils
- 2 tablespoons oil
- 1 onion, chopped
- 1 tomato, chopped
- 1/2 teaspoon ginger paste
- 1/2 teaspoon garlic paste
- 1/2 teaspoon cumin seeds
- 1/2 teaspoon turmeric powder
- 1/2 teaspoon red chili powder
- 1/2 teaspoon coriander powder
- 1/2 teaspoon garam masala
- Salt to taste
- 1/2 cup frozen peas
- 1/2 cup chopped cilantro

Instructions:

1. Wash the rice and lentils together and drain any excess water. Set aside.

2. In a large pan, heat the oil over medium heat.

3. Add the onion and cook until golden brown, about 5 minutes.

4. Add the tomato, ginger paste, garlic paste, cumin seeds, turmeric powder, red chili powder, coriander powder, garam masala, and salt to the pan. Cook until the tomato is soft and the spices are fragrant, about 5 minutes.

5. Add the rice and lentils to the pan and mix well with the spice mixture.

6. Add enough water to the pan to cover the rice and lentils by about 1 inch. Bring the mixture to a boil, then reduce the heat to low, cover the pan with a lid, and let simmer for 15-20 minutes, or until the rice and lentils are fully cooked and the liquid is absorbed.

7. Stir in the frozen peas and cilantro and cook for an additional 5 minutes.

8. Serve the bhuna khichuri hot as a main dish or side dish.

MOROG POLAO (CHICKEN AND RICE DISH)

Ingredients:

- 1 cup rice
- 1 pound boneless chicken, cut into bite-sized pieces
- 2 tablespoons oil
- 1 onion, chopped
- 1/2 teaspoon ginger paste
- 1/2 teaspoon garlic paste
- 1/2 teaspoon cumin seeds
- 1/2 teaspoon turmeric powder
- 1/2 teaspoon red chili powder
- 1/2 teaspoon coriander powder
- 1/2 teaspoon garam masala
- Salt to taste
- 1/2 cup frozen peas
- 1/2 cup chopped cilantro

Instructions:

1. Wash the rice and set aside.

2. In a large pan, heat the oil over medium heat.

3. Add the onion and cook until golden brown, about 5 minutes.

4. Add the chicken to the pan and cook until browned on all sides, about 5 minutes.

5. Add the ginger paste, garlic paste, cumin seeds, turmeric powder, red chili powder, coriander powder, garam masala, and salt to the pan. Cook until the spices are fragrant, about 5 minutes.

6. Add the rice to the pan and mix well with the chicken and spice mixture.

7. Add enough water to the pan to cover the rice by about 1 inch. Bring the mixture to a boil, then reduce the heat to low, cover the pan with a lid, and let simmer for 15-20 minutes, or until the rice is fully cooked and the liquid is absorbed.

8. Stir in the frozen peas and cilantro and cook for an additional 5 minutes.

9. Serve the morog polao hot as a main dish or side dish.

KALA BHUNA POLAO (BEEF AND RICE DISH)

Ingredients:

- 1 cup rice
- 1 pound beef, cut into bite-sized pieces
- 2 tablespoons oil

- 1 onion, chopped
- 1/2 teaspoon ginger paste
- 1/2 teaspoon garlic paste
- 1/2 teaspoon cumin seeds
- 1/2 teaspoon turmeric powder
- 1/2 teaspoon red chili powder
- 1/2 teaspoon coriander powder
- 1/2 teaspoon garam masala
- Salt to taste
- 1/2 cup frozen peas
- 1/2 cup chopped cilantro

Instructions:

1. Wash the rice and set aside.

2. In a large pan, heat the oil over medium heat.

3. Add the onion and cook until golden brown, about 5 minutes.

4. Add the beef to the pan and cook until browned on all sides, about 5 minutes.

5. Add the ginger paste, garlic paste, cumin seeds, turmeric powder, red chili powder, coriander powder, garam masala, and salt to the pan. Cook until the spices are fragrant, about 5 minutes.

6. Add the rice to the pan and mix well with the beef and spice mixture.

7. Add enough water to the pan to cover the rice by about 1 inch. Bring the mixture to a boil, then reduce the heat to low, cover the pan with a lid, and let simmer for 15-20 minutes, or until the rice is fully cooked and the liquid is absorbed.

8. Stir in the frozen peas and cilantro and cook for an additional 5 minutes.

9. Serve the kala bhuna polao hot as a main dish or side dish.

ILISH POLAO (HILSA FISH AND RICE DISH)

Ingredients:

- 1 cup rice
- 1 pound Hilsa fish, cut into bite-sized pieces
- 2 tablespoons oil
- 1 onion, chopped
- 1/2 teaspoon ginger paste
- 1/2 teaspoon garlic paste
- 1/2 teaspoon cumin seeds
- 1/2 teaspoon turmeric powder
- 1/2 teaspoon red chili powder
- 1/2 teaspoon coriander powder
- 1/2 teaspoon garam masala
- Salt to taste
- 1/2 cup frozen peas
- 1/2 cup chopped cilantro

Instructions:

1. Wash the rice and set aside.

2. In a large pan, heat the oil over medium heat.

3. Add the onion and cook until golden brown, about 5 minutes.

4. Add the Hilsa fish to the pan and cook until browned on both sides, about 5 minutes.

5. Add the ginger paste, garlic paste, cumin seeds, turmeric powder, red chili powder, coriander powder, garam masala, and salt to the pan. Cook until the spices are fragrant, about 5 minutes.

6. Add the rice to the pan and mix well with the fish and spice mixture.

7. Add enough water to the pan to cover the rice by about 1 inch. Bring the mixture to a boil, then reduce the heat to low, cover the pan with a lid, and let simmer for 15-20 minutes, or until the rice is fully cooked and the liquid is absorbed.

8. Stir in the frozen peas and cilantro and cook for an additional 5 minutes.

9. Serve the ilish polao hot as a main dish or side dish.

SHORSHE BATA ILISH
(HILSA FISH IN MUSTARD SAUCE)

Ingredients:

- 1 pound Hilsa fish, cut into bite-sized pieces
- 2 tablespoons mustard oil
- 1/2 teaspoon mustard seeds
- 1/2 teaspoon cumin seeds
- 1/2 teaspoon turmeric powder
- 1/2 teaspoon red chili powder
- 1/2 teaspoon coriander powder
- 1/2 teaspoon garam masala
- Salt to taste
- 1/2 cup mustard sauce
- 1/2 cup chopped cilantro

Instructions:

1. In a large pan, heat the mustard oil over medium heat.

2. Add the mustard seeds and cumin seeds to the pan and cook until fragrant, about 1 minute.

3. Add the Hilsa fish to the pan and cook until browned on both sides, about 5 minutes.

4. Add the turmeric powder, red chili powder, coriander powder, garam masala, and salt to the pan. Cook until the spices are fragrant, about 2 minutes.

5. Stir in the mustard sauce and cilantro and cook for an additional 2 minutes.

6. Serve the shorshe bata ilish hot as a main dish or side dish.

CHINGRI POLAO (SHRIMP AND RICE DISH)

Ingredients:

- 1 cup rice
- 1 pound shrimp, peeled and deveined
- 2 tablespoons oil
- 1 onion, chopped
- 1/2 teaspoon ginger paste
- 1/2 teaspoon garlic paste
- 1/2 teaspoon cumin seeds
- 1/2 teaspoon turmeric powder
- 1/2 teaspoon red chili powder
- 1/2 teaspoon coriander powder
- 1/2 teaspoon garam masala
- Salt to taste
- 1/2 cup frozen peas
- 1/2 cup chopped cilantro

Instructions:

1. Wash the rice and set aside.

2. In a large pan, heat the oil over medium heat.

3. Add the onion and cook until golden brown, about 5 minutes.

4. Add the shrimp to the pan and cook until pink on both sides, about 5 minutes.

5. Add the ginger paste, garlic paste, cumin seeds, turmeric powder, red chili powder, coriander powder, garam masala, and salt to the pan. Cook until the spices are fragrant, about 5 minutes.

6. Add the rice to the pan and mix well with the shrimp and spice mixture.

7. Add enough water to the pan to cover the rice by about 1 inch. Bring the mixture to a boil, then reduce the heat to low, cover the pan with a lid, and let simmer for 15-20 minutes, or until the rice is fully cooked and the liquid is absorbed.

8. Stir in the frozen peas and cilantro and cook for an additional 5 minutes.

9. Serve the chingri polao hot as a main dish or side dish.

MISHTI POLAO (SWEET RICE)

Ingredients:

- 1 cup rice
- 2 tablespoons ghee
- 1/2 cup sugar
- 1/2 teaspoon cardamom powder
- 1/2 cup raisins
- 1/2 cup chopped cashews

Instructions:

1. Wash the rice and set aside.

2. In a large pan, heat the ghee over medium heat.

3. Add the sugar, cardamom powder, raisins, and cashews to the pan and cook until the sugar is melted and the nuts are golden brown, about 5 minutes.

4. Add the rice to the pan and mix well with the sweet mixture.

5. Add enough water to the pan to cover the rice by about 1 inch. Bring the mixture to a boil, then reduce the heat to low, cover the pan with a lid, and let simmer for 15 -20 minutes, or until the rice is fully cooked and the liquid is absorbed.

6. Serve the mishti polao hot as a dessert or sweet side dish.

KICHURI (RICE AND LENTIL DISH)

Ingredients:

- 1 cup rice
- 1/2 cup yellow split peas
- 2 tablespoons oil
- 1 onion, chopped
- 1/2 teaspoon ginger paste
- 1/2 teaspoon garlic paste
- 1/2 teaspoon cumin seeds
- 1/2 teaspoon turmeric powder
- 1/2 teaspoon red chili powder
- 1/2 teaspoon coriander powder
- 1/2 teaspoon garam masala
- Salt to taste
- 1/2 cup frozen peas
- 1/2 cup chopped cilantro

Instructions:

1. Wash the rice and yellow split peas and set aside.

2. In a large pan, heat the oil over medium heat.

3. Add the onion and cook until golden brown, about 5 minutes.

4. Add the ginger paste, garlic paste, cumin seeds, turmeric powder, red chili powder, coriander powder, garam masala, and salt to the pan. Cook until the spices are fragrant, about 5 minutes.

5. Add the rice and yellow split peas to the pan and mix well with the spice mixture.

6. Add enough water to the pan to cover the rice and lentils by about 1 inch. Bring the mixture to a boil, then reduce the heat to low, cover the pan with a lid, and let simmer for 15-20 minutes, or until the rice and lentils are fully cooked and the liquid is absorbed.

7. Stir in the frozen peas and cilantro and cook for an additional 5 minutes.

8. Serve the kichuri hot as a main dish or side dish.

PANTA BHAT (FERMENTED RICE)

Ingredients:

- 2 cups rice
- 4 cups water
- 1 teaspoon salt

Instructions:

1. Wash the rice and set aside.

2. In a large bowl, mix the rice, water, and salt together.

3. Cover the bowl with a lid or plastic wrap and let the mixture ferment at room temperature for 12-24 hours.

4. Once fermented, the mixture will have a sour and tangy flavor. Serve the panta bhat as a snack or side dish.

KHICHDI (RICE AND LENTIL PORRIDGE)

Ingredients:

- 1 cup rice
- 1/2 cup yellow split peas
- 2 tablespoons oil
- 1 onion, chopped
- 1/2 teaspoon ginger paste
- 1/2 teaspoon garlic paste
- 1/2 teaspoon cumin seeds
- 1/2 teaspoon turmeric powder
- 1/2 teaspoon red chili powder
- 1/2 teaspoon coriander powder
- 1/2 teaspoon garam masala
- Salt to taste
- 1/2 cup frozen peas
- 1/2 cup chopped cilantro

Instructions:

1. Wash the rice and yellow split peas and set aside.

2. In a large pan, heat the oil over medium heat.

3. Add the onion and cook until golden brown, about 5 minutes.

4. Add the ginger paste, garlic paste, cumin seeds, turmeric powder, red chili powder, coriander powder, garam masala, and salt to the pan. Cook until the spices are fragrant, about 5 minutes.

5. Add the rice and yellow split peas to the pan and mix well with the spice mixture.

6. Add 4 cups of water to the pan and bring the mixture to a boil. Reduce the heat to low, cover the pan with a lid, and let simmer for 15-20 minutes, or until the rice and lentils are fully cooked and the liquid has been absorbed, creating a porridge-like consistency.

7. Stir in the frozen peas and cilantro and cook for an additional 5 minutes.

8. Serve the khichdi hot as a main dish or comfort food.

CURRIES AND STEWS

DHANSAAK

Ingredients:

- 1 pound lamb, cubed
- 1 cup yellow split peas
- 2 tablespoons oil
- 1 onion, chopped
- 1/2 teaspoon ginger paste
- 1/2 teaspoon garlic paste
- 1/2 teaspoon cumin seeds
- 1/2 teaspoon turmeric powder
- 1/2 teaspoon red chili powder
- 1/2 teaspoon coriander powder
- 1/2 teaspoon garam masala
- Salt to taste
- 1/2 cup chopped cilantro

Instructions:

1. Wash the yellow split peas and set aside.

2. In a large pan, heat the oil over medium heat.

3. Add the onion and cook until golden brown, about 5 minutes.

4. Add the ginger paste, garlic paste, cumin seeds, turmeric powder, red chili powder, coriander powder, garam masala, and salt to the pan. Cook until the spices are fragrant, about 5 minutes.

5. Add the lamb to the pan and cook until browned on all sides, about 10 minutes.

6. Add the yellow split peas to the pan and mix well with the lamb and spice mixture.

7. Add enough water to the pan to cover the lamb and split peas by about 1 inch. Bring the mixture to a boil, then reduce the heat to low, cover the pan with a lid, and let simmer for 45-60 minutes, or until the lamb is tender and the split peas are fully cooked.

8. Stir in the cilantro and cook for an additional 5 minutes.

9. Serve the dhansaak hot as a main dish with rice or bread.

DAL MAKHANI

Ingredients:

- 1 cup black lentils
- 1/2 cup red kidney beans
- 2 tablespoons oil
- 1 onion, chopped
- 1/2 teaspoon ginger paste
- 1/2 teaspoon garlic paste
- 1/2 teaspoon cumin seeds
- 1/2 teaspoon turmeric powder
- 1/2 teaspoon red chili powder
- 1/2 teaspoon coriander powder
- 1/2 teaspoon garam masala
- Salt to taste
- 1/2 cup chopped cilantro
- 1 cup heavy cream

Instructions:

1. Wash the black lentils and red kidney beans and set aside.

2. In a large pan, heat the oil over medium heat.

3. Add the onion and cook until golden brown, about 5 minutes.

4. Add the ginger paste, garlic paste, cumin seeds, turmeric powder, red chili powder, coriander powder, garam masala, and salt to the pan. Cook until the spices are fragrant, about 5 minutes.

5. Add the black lentils, red kidney beans, and enough water to cover the lentils and beans by about 1 inch to the pan. Bring the mixture to a boil, then reduce the heat to low, cover the pan with a lid, and let simmer for 45-60 minutes, or until the lentils and beans are fully cooked and soft.

6. Stir in the cilantro and heavy cream and cook for an additional 5-10 minutes, until the cream is fully incorporated into the mixture.

7. Serve the dal makhani hot as a main dish with rice or bread.

TARKA DAL

Ingredients:

- 1 cup yellow split peas
- 2 tablespoons oil
- 1 onion, chopped
- 1/2 teaspoon ginger paste
- 1/2 teaspoon garlic paste
- 1/2 teaspoon cumin seeds
- 1/2 teaspoon turmeric powder
- 1/2 teaspoon red chili powder
- 1/2 teaspoon coriander powder
- 1/2 teaspoon garam masala
- Salt to taste
- 1/2 cup chopped cilantro

Instructions:

1. Wash the yellow split peas and set aside.

2. In a large pan, heat the oil over medium heat.

3. Add the onion and cook until golden brown, about 5 minutes.

4. Add the ginger paste, garlic paste, cumin seeds, turmeric powder, red chili powder, coriander powder, garam masala, and salt to the pan. Cook until the spices are fragrant, about 5 minutes.

5. Add the yellow split peas and enough water to cover the split peas by about 1 inch to the pan. Bring the mixture to a boil, then reduce the heat to low, cover the pan with a lid, and let simmer for 45-60 minutes, or until the split peas are fully cooked and soft.

6. Stir in the cilantro and cook for an additional 5 minutes.

7. Serve the tarka dal hot as a main dish with rice or bread.

CHANA DAL

Ingredients:

- 1 cup split chickpeas
- 2 tablespoons oil
- 1 onion, chopped
- 1/2 teaspoon ginger paste
- 1/2 teaspoon garlic paste
- 1/2 teaspoon cumin seeds
- 1/2 teaspoon turmeric powder
- 1/2 teaspoon red chili powder
- 1/2 teaspoon coriander powder
- 1/2 teaspoon garam masala

- Salt to taste
- 1/2 cup chopped cilantro

Instructions:

1. Wash the split chickpeas and set aside.

2. In a large pan, heat the oil over medium heat.

3. Add the onion and cook until golden brown, about 5 minutes.

4. Add the ginger paste, garlic paste, cumin seeds, turmeric powder, red chili powder, coriander powder, garam masala, and salt to the pan. Cook until the spices are fragrant, about 5 minutes.

5. Add the split chickpeas and enough water to cover the chickpeas by about 1 inch to the pan. Bring the mixture to a boil, then reduce the heat to low, cover the pan with a lid, and let simmer for 45-60 minutes, or until the chickpeas are fully cooked and soft.

6. Stir in the cilantro and cook for an additional 5 minutes.

7. Serve the chana dal hot as a main dish with rice or bread.

MASOOR DAL

Ingredients:

- 1 cup red lentils
- 2 tablespoons oil
- 1 onion, chopped
- 1/2 teaspoon ginger paste
- 1/2 teaspoon garlic paste
- 1/2 teaspoon cumin seeds

- 1/2 teaspoon turmeric powder
- 1/2 teaspoon red chili powder
- 1/2 teaspoon coriander powder
- 1/2 teaspoon garam masala
- Salt to taste
- 1/2 cup chopped cilantro

Instructions:

1. Wash the red lentils and set aside.

2. In a large pan, heat the oil over medium heat.

3. Add the onion and cook until golden brown, about 5 minutes.

4. Add the ginger paste, garlic paste, cumin seeds, turmeric powder, red chili powder, coriander powder, garam masala, and salt to the pan. Cook until the spices are fragrant, about 5 minutes.

5. Add the red lentils and enough water to cover the lentils by about 1 inch to the pan. Bring the mixture to a boil, then reduce the heat to low, cover the pan with a lid, and let simmer for 45-60 minutes, or until the lentils are fully cooked and soft.

6. Stir in the cilantro and cook for an additional 5 minutes.

7. Serve the masoor dal hot as a main dish with rice or bread.

BEEF BHUNA

Ingredients:

- 1 lb beef, diced
- 2 tablespoons oil
- 1 onion, chopped

- 1/2 teaspoon ginger paste
- 1/2 teaspoon garlic paste
- 1/2 teaspoon cumin seeds
- 1/2 teaspoon turmeric powder
- 1/2 teaspoon red chili powder
- 1/2 teaspoon coriander powder
- 1/2 teaspoon garam masala
- Salt to taste
- 1/2 cup chopped cilantro

Instructions:

1. In a large pan, heat the oil over medium heat.

2. Add the onion and cook until golden brown, about 5 minutes.

3. Add the ginger paste, garlic paste, cumin seeds, turmeric powder, red chili powder, coriander powder, garam masala, and salt to the pan. Cook until the spices are fragrant, about 5 minutes.

4. Add the diced beef to the pan and cook until browned, about 5-7 minutes.

5. Add enough water to cover the beef by about 1 inch to the pan. Bring the mixture to a boil, then reduce the heat to low, cover the pan with a lid, and let simmer for 45-60 minutes, or until the beef is fully cooked and tender.

6. Stir in the cilantro and cook for an additional 5 minutes.

7. Serve the beef bhuna hot as a main dish with rice or bread.

CHICKEN KORMA

Ingredients:

- 1 lb chicken, diced
- 2 tablespoons oil
- 1 onion, chopped
- 1/2 teaspoon ginger paste
- 1/2 teaspoon garlic paste
- 1/2 teaspoon cumin seeds
- 1/2 teaspoon turmeric powder
- 1/2 teaspoon red chili powder
- 1/2 teaspoon coriander powder
- 1/2 teaspoon garam masala
- 1/2 cup plain yogurt
- Salt to taste
- 1/2 cup chopped cilantro

Instructions:

1. In a large pan, heat the oil over medium heat.

2. Add the onion and cook until golden brown, about 5 minutes.

3. Add the ginger paste, garlic paste, cumin seeds, turmeric powder, red chili powder, coriander powder, garam masala, and salt to the pan. Cook until the spices are fragrant, about 5 minutes.

4. Add the diced chicken to the pan and cook until browned, about 5-7 minutes.

5. Stir in the yogurt and enough water to cover the chicken by about 1 inch to the pan. Bring the mixture to a boil, then reduce the heat to low, cover the pan with a lid, and let simmer for 45-60 minutes, or until the chicken is fully cooked and tender.

6. Stir in the cilantro and cook for an additional 5 minutes.

7. Serve the chicken korma hot as a main dish with rice or bread.

CHICKEN JALFREZI

Ingredients:

- 1 lb chicken, diced
- 2 tablespoons oil
- 1 onion, chopped
- 1/2 teaspoon ginger paste
- 1/2 teaspoon garlic paste
- 1/2 teaspoon cumin seeds
- 1/2 teaspoon turmeric powder
- 1/2 teaspoon red chili powder
- 1/2 teaspoon coriander powder
- 1/2 teaspoon garam masala
- 1/2 cup chopped bell peppers
- 1/2 cup chopped tomatoes
- Salt to taste
- 1/2 cup chopped cilantro

Instructions:

1. In a large pan, heat the oil over medium heat.

2. Add the onion and cook until golden brown, about 5 minutes.

3. Add the ginger paste, garlic paste, cumin seeds, turmeric powder, red chili powder, coriander powder, garam masala, and salt to the pan. Cook until the spices are fragrant, about 5 minutes.

4. Add the diced chicken to the pan and cook until browned, about 5-7 minutes.

5. Stir in the bell peppers, tomatoes, and enough water to cover the chicken by about 1 inch to the pan. Bring the mixture to a boil, then reduce the heat to low, cover the pan with a lid, and let simmer for 45-60 minutes, or until the chicken is fully cooked and tender.

6. Stir in the cilantro and cook for an additional 5 minutes.

7. Serve the chicken jalfrezi hot as a main dish with rice or bread.

MUTTON REZALA

Ingredients:

- 1 lb mutton, diced
- 2 tablespoons oil
- 1 onion, chopped
- 1/2 teaspoon ginger paste
- 1/2 teaspoon garlic paste
- 1/2 teaspoon cumin seeds

<

- 1/2 teaspoon turmeric powder
- 1/2 teaspoon red chili powder
- 1/2 teaspoon coriander powder
- 1/2 teaspoon garam masala
- 1/2 cup plain yogurt
- Salt to taste
- 1/2 cup chopped cilantro

Instructions:

1. In a large pan, heat the oil over medium heat.

2. Add the onion and cook until golden brown, about 5 minutes.

3. Add the ginger paste, garlic paste, cumin seeds, turmeric powder, red chili powder, coriander powder, garam masala, and salt to the pan. Cook until the spices are fragrant, about 5 minutes.

4. Add the diced mutton to the pan and cook until browned, about 5-7 minutes.

5. Stir in the yogurt and enough water to cover the mutton by about 1 inch to the pan. Bring the mixture to a boil, then reduce the heat to low, cover the pan with a lid, and let simmer for 45-60 minutes, or until the mutton is fully cooked and tender.

6. Stir in the cilantro and cook for an additional 5 minutes.

7. Serve the mutton rezala hot as a main dish with rice or bread.

KOSHA MANGSHO (SLOW-COOKED MEAT)

Ingredients:

- 1 lb beef, diced
- 2 tablespoons oil
- 1 onion, chopped
- 1/2 teaspoon ginger paste
- 1/2 teaspoon garlic paste
- 1/2 teaspoon cumin seeds
- 1/2 teaspoon turmeric powder
- 1/2 teaspoon red chili powder
- 1/2 teaspoon coriander powder
- 1/2 teaspoon garam masala
- 1 cup plain yogurt
- Salt to taste
- 1/2 cup chopped cilantro

Instructions:

1. In a large pan, heat the oil over medium heat.

2. Add the onion and cook until golden brown, about 5 minutes.

3. Add the ginger paste, garlic paste, cumin seeds, turmeric powder, red chili powder, coriander powder, garam masala, and salt to the pan. Cook until the spices are fragrant, about 5 minutes.

4. Add the diced beef to the pan and cook until browned, about 5-7 minutes.

5. Stir in the yogurt and enough water to cover the beef by about 1 inch to the pan. Bring the mixture to a boil, then reduce the heat to low, cover the pan with a lid, and let simmer for 2-3 hours, or until the beef is fully cooked and tender.

6. Stir in the cilantro and cook for an additional 5 minutes.

7. Serve the kosha mangsho hot as a main dish with rice or bread.

CHICKEN BHARTA

Ingredients:

- 1 lb chicken, diced
- 2 tablespoons oil
- 1 onion, chopped
- 1/2 teaspoon ginger paste
- 1/2 teaspoon garlic paste
- 1/2 teaspoon cumin seeds
- 1/2 teaspoon turmeric powder
- 1/2 teaspoon red chili powder
- 1/2 teaspoon coriander powder

- 1/2 teaspoon garam masala
- 1 cup plain yogurt
- Salt to taste
- 1/2 cup chopped cilantro

Instructions:

1. In a large pan, heat the oil over medium heat.

2. Add the onion and cook until golden brown, about 5 minutes.

3. Add the ginger paste, garlic paste, cumin seeds, turmeric powder, red chili powder, coriander powder, garam masala, and salt to the pan. Cook until the spices are fragrant, about 5 minutes.

4. Add the diced chicken to the pan and cook until browned, about 5-7 minutes.

5. Stir in the yogurt and enough water to cover the chicken by about 1 inch to the pan. Bring the mixture to a boil, then reduce the heat to low, cover the pan with a lid, and let simmer for 45-60 minutes, or until the chicken is fully cooked and tender.

6. Remove the chicken from the pan and shred it using two forks. Set aside.

7. In the same pan, add the shredded chicken back in and cook until the sauce has thickened, about 10 minutes.

8. Stir in the cilantro and cook for an additional 5 minutes.

9. Serve the chicken bharta hot as a main dish with rice or bread.

MURGHI MASALLAM
(WHOLE CHICKEN CURRY)

Ingredients:

- 1 whole chicken, cleaned and cut into pieces
- 2 tablespoons oil
- 1 onion, chopped
- 1/2 teaspoon ginger paste
- 1/2 teaspoon garlic paste
- 1/2 teaspoon cumin seeds
- 1/2 teaspoon turmeric powder
- 1/2 teaspoon red chili powder
- 1/2 teaspoon coriander powder
- 1/2 teaspoon garam masala
- 1 cup plain yogurt
- Salt to taste
- 1/2 cup chopped cilantro

Instructions:

1. In a large pan, heat the oil over medium heat.

2. Add the onion and cook until golden brown, about 5 minutes.

3. Add the ginger paste, garlic paste, cumin seeds, turmeric powder, red chili powder, coriander powder, garam masala, and salt to the pan. Cook until the spices are fragrant, about 5 minutes.

4. Add the chicken pieces to the pan and cook until browned, about 5-7 minutes on each side.

5. Stir in the yogurt and enough water to cover the chicken by about 1 inch to the pan. Bring the mixture to a boil, then reduce the heat to low, cover the pan with a lid, and let simmer for 45-60 minutes, or until the chicken is fully cooked and tender.

6. Stir in the cilantro and cook for an additional 5 minutes.

7. Serve the murghi masallam hot as a main dish with rice or bread.

SHOBJI DAL
(MIXED VEGETABLE AND LENTIL CURRY)

Ingredients:

- 1 cup mixed vegetables (such as carrots, green beans, and potatoes), chopped
- 1 cup yellow split peas
- 2 tablespoons oil
- 1 onion, chopped
- 1/2 teaspoon ginger paste
- 1/2 teaspoon garlic paste
- 1/2 teaspoon cumin seeds
- 1/2 teaspoon turmeric powder
- 1/2 teaspoon red chili powder
- 1/2 teaspoon coriander powder
- 1/2 teaspoon garam masala
- Salt to taste
- 1/2 cup chopped cilantro

Instructions:

1. Rinse the yellow split peas and let soak for 30 minutes.

2. In a large pan, heat the oil over medium heat.

3. Add the onion and cook until golden brown, about 5 minutes.

4. Add the ginger paste, garlic paste, cumin seeds, turmeric powder, red chili powder, coriander powder, garam masala, and salt to the pan. Cook until the spices are fragrant, about 5 minutes.

5. Add the mixed vegetables and drained yellow split peas to the pan. Stir to combine with the spices.

6. Add enough water to the pan to cover the vegetables and lentils by about 1 inch. Bring the mixture to a boil, then reduce the heat to low, cover the pan with a lid, and let simmer for 45-60 minutes, or until the vegetables and lentils are fully cooked and tender.

7. Stir in the cilantro and cook for an additional 5 minutes.

8. Serve the shobji dal hot as a main dish with rice or bread.

ECHORER DALNA (GREEN JACKFRUIT CURRY)

Ingredients:

- 1 lb green jackfruit, diced
- 2 tablespoons oil
- 1 onion, chopped
- 1/2 teaspoon ginger paste
- 1/2 teaspoon garlic paste
- 1/2 teaspoon cumin seeds
- 1/2 teaspoon turmeric powder
- 1/2 teaspoon red chili powder
- 1/2 teaspoon coriander powder
- 1/2 teaspoon garam masala
- 1 cup plain yogurt
- Salt to taste
- 1/2 cup chopped cilantro

Instructions:

1. In a large pan, heat the oil over medium heat.2. Add the onion and cook until golden brown, about 5 minutes.

3. Add the ginger paste, garlic paste, cumin seeds, turmeric powder, red chili powder, coriander powder, garam masala, and salt to the pan. Cook until the spices are fragrant, about 5 minutes.

4. Add the diced green jackfruit to the pan and cook until tender, about 10-15 minutes.

5. Stir in the yogurt and enough water to cover the jackfruit by about 1 inch to the pan. Bring the mixture to a boil, then reduce the heat to low, cover the pan with a lid, and let simmer for 45-60 minutes, or until the jackfruit is fully cooked and the sauce has thickened.

6. Stir in the cilantro and cook for an additional 5 minutes.

7. Serve the echorer dalna hot as a main dish with rice or bread.

LAU CHINGRI
(BOTTLE GOURD AND SHRIMP CURRY)

Ingredients:

- 1 lb bottle gourd, peeled and diced
- 1 lb shrimp, peeled and deveined
- 2 tablespoons oil
- 1 onion, chopped
- 1/2 teaspoon ginger paste
- 1/2 teaspoon garlic paste
- 1/2 teaspoon cumin seeds
- 1/2 teaspoon turmeric powder

- 1/2 teaspoon red chili powder
- 1/2 teaspoon coriander powder
- 1/2 teaspoon garam masala
- 1 cup coconut milk
- Salt to taste
- 1/2 cup chopped cilantro

Instructions:

1. In a large pan, heat the oil over medium heat.

2. Add the onion and cook until golden brown, about 5 minutes.

3. Add the ginger paste, garlic paste, cumin seeds, turmeric powder, red chili powder, coriander powder, garam masala, and salt to the pan. Cook until the spices are fragrant, about 5 minutes.

4. Add the diced bottle gourd to the pan and cook until tender, about 10-15 minutes.

5. Stir in the coconut milk and enough water to cover the gourd by about 1 inch to the pan. Bring the mixture to a boil, then reduce the heat to low, cover the pan with a lid, and let simmer for 45-60 minutes, or until the gourd is fully cooked and the sauce has thickened.

6. Add the shrimp to the pan and cook until pink, about 5-7 minutes.

7. Stir in the cilantro and cook for an additional 5 minutes.

8. Serve the lau chingri hot as a main dish with rice or bread.

ALU VORTA (MASHED POTATO)

Ingredients:

- 4 large potatoes, peeled and diced
- 2 tablespoons oil
- 1 onion, chopped
- 1/2 teaspoon ginger paste
- 1/2 teaspoon garlic paste
- 1/2 teaspoon cumin seeds
- 1/2 teaspoon turmeric powder
- 1/2 teaspoon red chili powder
- 1/2 teaspoon coriander powder
- 1/2 teaspoon garam masala
- Salt to taste
- 1/2 cup chopped cilantro

Instructions:

1. Boil the diced potatoes in a pot of salted water until tender, about 15-20 minutes.

2. Drain the potatoes and mash with a fork or potato masher until smooth.

3. In a large pan, heat the oil over medium heat.

4. Add the onion and cook until golden brown, about 5 minutes.

5. Add the ginger paste, garlic paste, cumin seeds, turmeric powder, red chili powder, coriander powder, garam masala, and salt to the pan. Cook until the spices are fragrant, about 5 minutes.

6. Stir in the mashed potatoes and cook for an additional 5-7 minutes, stirring occasionally.

7. Stir in the cilantro and cook for an additional 5 minutes.

8. Serve the alu vorta hot as a side dish or as a filling for sandwiches or wraps.

BAINGAN BHARTA (MASHED EGGPLANT)

Ingredients:

- 2 large eggplants
- 2 tablespoons oil
- 1 onion, chopped
- 1/2 teaspoon ginger paste
- 1/2 teaspoon garlic paste
- 1/2 teaspoon cumin seeds
- 1/2 teaspoon turmeric powder
- 1/2 teaspoon red chili powder
- 1/2 teaspoon coriander powder
- 1/2 teaspoon garam masala
- Salt to taste
- 1/2 cup chopped cilantro

Instructions:

1. Roast the eggplants over an open flame until the skin is charred and the flesh is soft, about 10-15 minutes. Alternatively, bake the eggplants in a 400°F oven for 30-35 minutes.

2. Peel the charred skin from the eggplants and mash the flesh with a fork or potato masher until smooth.

3. In a large pan, heat the oil over medium heat.

4. Add the onion and cook until golden brown, about 5 minutes.

5. Add the ginger paste, garlic paste, cumin seeds, turmeric powder, red chili powder, coriander powder, garam masala, and salt to the pan. Cook until the spices are fragrant, about 5 minutes.

6. Stir in the mashed eggplant and cook for an additional 5-7 minutes, stirring occasionally.

7. Stir in the cilantro and cook for an additional 5 minutes.

8. Serve the baingan bharta hot as a side dish or as a filling for sandwiches or wraps.

SHUTKI BHORTA (DRIED FISH MASH)

Ingredients:

- 1 lb dried fish
- 2 tablespoons oil
- 1 onion, chopped
- 1/2 teaspoon ginger paste
- 1/2 teaspoon garlic paste
- 1/2 teaspoon cumin seeds
- 1/2 teaspoon turmeric powder
- 1/2 teaspoon red chili powder
- 1/2 teaspoon coriander powder
- 1/2 teaspoon garam masala
- Salt to taste
- 1/2 cup chopped cilantro

Instructions:

1. Soak the dried fish in water for 30 minutes to soften.

2. Drain the fish and grind to a coarse paste in a food processor or with a mortar and pestle.

3. In a large pan, heat the oil over medium heat.

4. Add the onion and cook until golden brown, about 5 minutes.

5. Add the ginger paste, garlic paste, cumin seeds, turmeric powder, red chili powder, coriander powder, garam masala, and salt to the pan. Cook until the spices are fragrant, about 5 minutes.

6. Stir in the ground dried fish and cook for an additional 5-7 minutes, stirring occasionally.

7. Stir in the cilantro and cook for an additional 5 minutes.

8. Serve the shutki bhorta hot as a side dish or as a filling for sandwiches or wraps.

SHOBJI BHORTA
(MIXED VEGETABLE MASH)

Ingredients:

- 1 lb mixed vegetables (such as potatoes, eggplants, pumpkins, or bottle gourd), peeled and diced
- 2 tablespoons oil
- 1 onion, chopped
- 1/2 teaspoon ginger paste
- 1/2 teaspoon garlic paste
- 1/2 teaspoon cumin seeds
- 1/2 teaspoon turmeric powder
- 1/2 teaspoon red chili powder
- 1/2 teaspoon coriander powder
- 1/2 teaspoon garam masala
- Salt to taste
- 1/2 cup chopped cilantro

Instructions:

1. Boil the diced vegetables in a pot of salted water until tender, about 15-20 minutes.

2. Drain the vegetables and mash with a fork or potato masher until smooth.

3. In a large pan, heat the oil over medium heat.

4. Add the onion and cook until golden brown, about 5 minutes.

5. Add the ginger paste, garlic paste, cumin seeds, turmeric powder, red chili powder, coriander powder, garam masala, and salt to the pan. Cook until the spices are fragrant, about 5 minutes.

6. Stir in the mashed vegetables and cook for an additional 5-7 minutes, stirring occasionally.

7. Stir in the cilantro and cook for an additional 5 minutes.

8. Serve the shobji bhorta hot as a side dish or as a filling for sandwiches or wraps.

BHINDI BHAJI (OKRA STIR-FRY)

Ingredients:

- 1 lb okra, trimmed and sliced
- 2 tablespoons oil
- 1 onion, chopped
- 1/2 teaspoon ginger paste
- 1/2 teaspoon garlic paste
- 1/2 teaspoon cumin seeds
- 1/2 teaspoon turmeric powder
- 1/2 teaspoon red chili powder
- 1/2 teaspoon coriander powder
- 1/2 teaspoon garam masala

- Salt to taste
- 1/2 cup chopped cilantro

Instructions:

1. In a large pan, heat the oil over medium heat.

2. Add the onion and cook until golden brown, about 5 minutes.

3. Add the ginger paste, garlic paste, cumin seeds, turmeric powder, red chili powder, coriander powder, garam masala, and salt to the pan. Cook until the spices are fragrant, about 5 minutes.

4. Stir in the sliced okra and cook for an additional 5-7 minutes, stirring occasionally.

5. Stir in the cilantro and cook for an additional 5 minutes.

6. Serve the bhindi bhaji hot as a side dish or as a filling for sandwiches or wraps.

NIRAMISH
(MIXED VEGETABLE CURRY)

Ingredients:

- 1 lb mixed vegetables (such as potatoes, eggplants, carrots, or bottle gourd), peeled and diced
- 2 tablespoons oil
- 1 onion, chopped
- 1/2 teaspoon ginger paste
- 1/2 teaspoon garlic paste
- 1/2 teaspoon cumin seeds
- 1/2 teaspoon turmeric powder
- 1/2 teaspoon red chili powder

- 1/2 teaspoon coriander powder
- 1/2 teaspoon garam masala
- Salt to taste
- 1/2 cup chopped cilantro
- 1 cup water

Instructions:

1. In a large pan, heat the oil over medium heat.

2. Add the onion and cook until golden brown, about 5 minutes.

3. Add the ginger paste, garlic paste, cumin seeds, turmeric powder, red chili powder, coriander powder, garam masala, and salt to the pan. Cook until the spices are fragrant, about 5 minutes.

4. Stir in the diced vegetables and cook for an additional 5-7 minutes, stirring occasionally.

5. Stir in the cilantro and cook for an additional 5 minutes.

6. Pour in the water and bring to a boil. Reduce heat to low and let the curry simmer for 10-15 minutes, or until the vegetables are tender.

7. Serve the niramish hot over rice or with bread as a main dish.

LABRA (MIXED VEGETABLE STEW)

Ingredients:

- 1 lb mixed vegetables (such as potatoes, eggplants, carrots, or bottle gourd), peeled and diced
- 2 tablespoons oil

- 1 onion, chopped
- 1/2 teaspoon ginger paste
- 1/2 teaspoon garlic paste
- 1/2 teaspoon cumin seeds
- 1/2 teaspoon turmeric powder
- 1/2 teaspoon red chili powder
- 1/2 teaspoon coriander powder
- 1/2 teaspoon garam masala
- Salt to taste
- 1/2 cup chopped cilantro
- 1 cup water

Instructions:

1. In a large pan, heat the oil over medium heat.

2. Add the onion and cook until golden brown, about 5 minutes.

3. Add the ginger paste, garlic paste, cumin seeds, turmeric powder, red chili powder, coriander powder, garam masala, and salt to the pan. Cook until the spices are fragrant, about 5 minutes.

4. Stir in the diced vegetables and cook for an additional 5-7 minutes, stirring occasionally.

5. Stir in the cilantro and cook for an additional 5 minutes.

6. Pour in the water and bring to a boil. Reduce heat to low and let the stew simmer for 10-15 minutes, or until the vegetables are tender.

7. Serve the labra hot over rice or with bread as a main dish.

CHORCHORI (MIXED VEGETABLE MEDLEY)

Ingredients:

- 1 lb mixed vegetables (such as potatoes, eggplants, carrots, or bottle gourd), peeled and diced
- 2 tablespoons oil
- 1 onion, chopped
- 1/2 teaspoon ginger paste
- 1/2 teaspoon garlic paste
- 1/2 teaspoon cumin seeds
- 1/2 teaspoon turmeric powder
- 1/2 teaspoon red chili powder
- 1/2 teaspoon coriander powder
- 1/2 teaspoon garam masalaSalt to taste
- 1/2 cup chopped cilantro
- 1 cup water

Instructions:

1. In a large pan, heat the oil over medium heat.

2. Add the onion and cook until golden brown, about 5 minutes.

3. Add the ginger paste, garlic paste, cumin seeds, turmeric powder, red chili powder, coriander powder, garam masala, and salt to the pan. Cook until the spices are fragrant, about 5 minutes.

4. Stir in the diced vegetables and cook for an additional 5-7 minutes, stirring occasionally.

5. Stir in the cilantro and cook for an additional 5 minutes.

6. Pour in the water and bring to a boil. Reduce heat to low and let the medley simmer for 10-15 minutes, or until the vegetables are tender.

7. Serve the chorchori hot over rice or with bread as a main dish.

PALONG SHAAK (SPINACH CURRY)

Ingredients:

- 1 lb spinach, chopped
- 2 tablespoons oil
- 1 onion, chopped
- 1/2 teaspoon ginger paste
- 1/2 teaspoon garlic paste
- 1/2 teaspoon cumin seeds
- 1/2 teaspoon turmeric powder
- 1/2 teaspoon red chili powder
- 1/2 teaspoon coriander powder
- 1/2 teaspoon garam masala
- Salt to taste
- 1/2 cup chopped cilantro
- 1 cup water

Instructions:

1. In a large pan, heat the oil over medium heat.

2. Add the onion and cook until golden brown, about 5 minutes.

3. Add the ginger paste, garlic paste, cumin seeds, turmeric powder, red chili powder, coriander powder, garam masala, and salt to the pan. Cook until the spices are fragrant, about 5 minutes.

4. Stir in the chopped spinach and cook for an additional 5-7 minutes, stirring occasionally.

5. Stir in the cilantro and cook for an additional 5 minutes.

6. Pour in the water and bring to a boil. Reduce heat to low and let the curry simmer for 10-15 minutes, or until the spinach is tender.

7. Serve the palong shaak hot over rice or with bread as a main dish.

SHAAK BHAJA (FRIED LEAFY GREENS)

Ingredients:

- 1 lb leafy greens (such as spinach or mustard greens), chopped
- 2 tablespoons oil
- 1/2 teaspoon salt

Instructions:

1. In a large pan, heat the oil over medium heat.

2. Stir in the chopped leafy greens and cook for 5-7 minutes, stirring occasionally, until the greens are wilted and tender.

3. Sprinkle salt over the greens and stir to combine.

4. Fry the greens until crispy and golden brown, about 5 minutes.

5. Serve the shaak bhaja as a snack or side dish.

CAULIFLOWER AND POTATO CURRY

Ingredients:

- 1 head cauliflower, chopped

- 2 potatoes, peeled and diced
- 2 tablespoons oil
- 1 onion, chopped
- 1/2 teaspoon ginger paste
- 1/2 teaspoon garlic paste
- 1/2 teaspoon cumin seeds
- 1/2 teaspoon turmeric powder
- 1/2 teaspoon red chili powder
- 1/2 teaspoon coriander powder
- 1/2 teaspoon garam masala
- Salt to taste
- 1/2 cup chopped cilantro
- 1 cup water

Instructions:

1. In a large pan, heat the oil over medium heat.

2. Add the onion and cook until golden brown, about 5 minutes.

3. Add the ginger paste, garlic paste, cumin seeds, turmeric powder, red chili powder, coriander powder, garam masala, and salt to the pan. Cook until the spices are fragrant, about 5 minutes.

4. Stir in the chopped cauliflower and diced potatoes and cook for an additional 5-7 minutes, stirring occasionally.

5. Stir in the cilantro and cook for an additional 5 minutes.

6. Pour in the water and bring to a boil. Reduce heat to low and let the curry simmer for 10-15 minutes, or until the vegetables are tender.

7. Serve the cauliflower and potato curry hot over rice or with bread as a main dish.

PUMPKIN AND SHRIMP CURRY

Ingredients:

- 1 lb pumpkin, peeled and diced
- 1 lb shrimp, peeled and deveined
- 2 tablespoons oil
- 1 onion, chopped
- 1/2 teaspoon ginger paste
- 1/2 teaspoon garlic paste
- 1/2 teaspoon cumin seeds
- 1/2 teaspoon turmeric powder
- 1/2 teaspoon red chili powder
- 1/2 teaspoon coriander powder
- 1/2 teaspoon garam masala
- Salt to taste
- 1/2 cup chopped cilantro
- 1 cup water

Instructions:

1. In a large pan, heat the oil over medium heat.

2. Add the onion and cook until golden brown, about 5 minutes.

3. Add the ginger paste, garlic paste, cumin seeds, turmeric powder, red chili powder, coriander powder, garam masala, and salt to the pan. Cook until the spices are fragrant, about 5 minutes.

4. Stir in the diced pumpkin and cook for an additional 5-7 minutes, stirring occasionally.

5. Add the shrimp to the pan and cook for an additional 5 minutes, or until the shrimp are pink and cooked through.

6. Stir in the cilantro and cook for an additional 5 minutes.

7. Pour in the water and bring to a boil. Reduce heat to low and let the curry simmer for 10-15 minutes, or until the pumpkin is tender.

8. Serve the pumpkin and shrimp curry hot over rice or with bread as a main dish.

FISH & SEAFOOD

MAACH BHAJA (FRIED FISH)

Ingredients:

- 1 lb fish fillets, cut into pieces
- 1 cup flour
- 1 teaspoon salt
- 1/2 teaspoon turmeric powder
- 1/2 teaspoon red chili powder
- 1/2 teaspoon coriander powder
- 1/2 teaspoon garam masala
- Oil for frying

Instructions:

1. In a bowl, mix together the flour, salt, turmeric powder, red chili powder, coriander powder, and garam masala.

2. Dredge the fish fillets in the flour mixture, making sure that each piece is well coated.

3. In a large pan, heat the oil over medium heat.

4. Fry the coated fish fillets until golden brown and crispy, about 5 minutes on each side.

5. Serve the maach bhaja hot as a snack or main dish.

DOI MAACH (FISH IN YOGURT SAUCE)

Ingredients:

- 1 lb fish fillets, cut into pieces
- 1 cup plain yogurt
- 1/2 teaspoon turmeric powder
- 1/2 teaspoon red chili powder
- 1/2 teaspoon coriander powder
- 1/2 teaspoon garam masala
- 1/2 teaspoon salt
- 1 onion, chopped
- 1/2 teaspoon ginger paste
- 1/2 teaspoon garlic paste
- 1/2 cup water

Instructions:

1. In a bowl, mix together the yogurt, turmeric powder, red chili powder, coriander powder, garam masala, and salt to create the marinade.

2. Place the fish fillets in the marinade and let sit for 30 minutes to an hour.

3. In a large pan, heat some oil over medium heat.

4. Add the onion and cook until golden brown, about 5 minutes.

5. Stir in the ginger paste, garlic paste, and the marinated fish fillets. Cook for 5-7 minutes, or until the fish is cooked through.

6. Pour in the water and bring to a boil. Reduce heat to low and let the curry simmer for 10-15 minutes, or until the sauce has thickened slightly.

7. Serve the doi maach hot over rice as a main dish.

RUI MAACHER JHOL (FISH CURRY)

Ingredients:

- 1 lb fish fillets, cut into pieces
- 2 tablespoons oil
- 1 onion, chopped
- 1/2 teaspoon ginger paste
- 1/2 teaspoon garlic paste
- 1/2 teaspoon cumin seeds
- 1/2 teaspoon turmeric powder
- 1/2 teaspoon red chili powder
- 1/2 teaspoon coriander powder
- 1/2 teaspoon garam masala
- Salt to taste
- 1/2 cup chopped cilantro
- 1 cup water

Instructions:

1. In a large pan, heat the oil over medium heat.

2. Add the onion and cook until golden brown, about 5 minutes.

3. Add the ginger paste, garlic paste, cumin seeds, turmeric powder, red chili powder, coriander powder, garam masala, and salt to the pan. Cook until the spices are fragrant, about 5 minutes.

4. Stir in the fish fillets and cook for an additional 5-7 minutes, or until the fish is cooked through.

5. Stir in the cilantro and cook for an additional 5 minutes.

6. Pour in the water and bring to a boil. Reduce heat to low and let the curry simmer for 10-15 minutes, or until the sauce has thickened slightly.

7. Serve the rui maacher jhol hot over rice as a main dish.

ILISH BHAJA (FRIED HILSA FISH)

Ingredients:

- 1 lb Hilsa fish fillets, cut into pieces
- 1 cup flour
- 1 teaspoon salt
- 1/2 teaspoon turmeric powder
- 1/2 teaspoon red chili powder
- 1/2 teaspoon coriander powder
- 1/2 teaspoon garam masala
- Oil for frying

Instructions:

1. In a bowl, mix together the flour, salt, turmeric powder, red chili powder, coriander powder, and garam masala.

2. Dredge the Hilsa fish fillets in the flour mixture, making sure that each piece is well coated.

3. In a large pan, heat the oil over medium heat.

4. Fry the coated Hilsa fish fillets until golden brown and crispy, about 5 minutes on each side.

5. Serve the ilish bhaja hot as a snack or main dish.

SHORSHE ILISH (HILSA FISH IN MUSTARD SAUCE)

Ingredients:

- 1 lb Hilsa fish fillets, cut into pieces
- 1/2 cup mustard seeds
- 1/2 cup water
- 1/2 teaspoon turmeric powder

- 1/2 teaspoon red chili powder
- 1/2 teaspoon coriander powder
- 1/2 teaspoon garam masala
- 1/2 teaspoon salt
- 1 onion, chopped
- 1/2 teaspoon ginger paste
- 1/2 teaspoon garlic paste

Instructions:

1. In a blender, blend together the mustard seeds and water until smooth.

2. In a large pan, heat some oil over medium heat.

3. Add the onion and cook until golden brown, about 5 minutes.

4. Stir in the ginger paste, garlic paste, turmeric powder, red chili powder, coriander powder, garam masala, and salt. Cook until the spices are fragrant, about 5 minutes.

5. Stir in the blended mustard sauce and bring to a boil. Reduce heat to low and let the sauce simmer for 10 minutes.

6. Add the Hilsa fish fillets to the pan and let simmer until the fish is cooked through, about 10-15 minutes.

7. Serve the shorshe ilish hot over rice as a main dish.

PABDA MACHER JHAL (PABDA FISH CURRY)

Ingredients:

- 1 lb Pabda fish fillets, cut into pieces
- 2 tablespoons oil

- 1 onion, chopped
- 1/2 teaspoon ginger paste
- 1/2 teaspoon garlic paste
- 1/2 teaspoon cumin seeds
- 1/2 teaspoon turmeric powder
- 1/2 teaspoon red chili powder
- 1/2 teaspoon coriander powder
- 1/2 teaspoon garam masala
- Salt to taste
- 1/2 cup chopped cilantro
- 1 cup water

Instructions:

1. In a large pan, heat the oil over medium heat.

2. Add the onion and cook until golden brown, about 5 minutes.

3. Add the ginger paste, garlic paste, cumin seeds, turmeric powder, red chili powder, coriander powder, garam masala, and salt to the pan. Cook until the spices are fragrant, about 5 minutes.

4. Stir in the Pabda fish fillets and cook for an additional 5-7 minutes, or until the fish is cooked through.

5. Stir in the cilantro and cook for an additional 5 minutes.

6. Pour in the water and bring to a boil. Reduce heat to low and let the curry simmer for 10-15 minutes, or until the sauce has thickened slightly.

7. Serve the pabda macher jhal hot over rice as a main dish.

CHITAL MACHER MUITHA
(FISH DUMPLINGS)

Ingredients:

- 1 lb fish fillets, finely chopped
- 1 cup flour
- 1/2 teaspoon salt
- 1/2 teaspoon turmeric powder
- 1/2 teaspoon red chili powder
- 1/2 teaspoon coriander powder
- 1/2 teaspoon garam masala
- 1 egg
- 1/2 cup chopped cilantro
- Oil for frying

Instructions:

1. In a bowl, mix together the chopped fish, flour, salt, turmeric powder, red chili powder, coriander powder, garam masala, egg, and cilantro.

2. Shape the mixture into small dumplings, about the size of a ping pong ball.

3. In a large pan, heat the oil over medium heat.

4. Fry the fish dumplings until golden brown and crispy, about 5 minutes on each side.

5. Serve the chital macher muitha hot as a snack or main dish.

KOI MACHER JHOL
(CLIMBING PERCH FISH CURRY)

Ingredients:

- 1 lb climbing perch fish fillets, cut into pieces
- 2 tablespoons oil
- 1 onion, chopped
- 1/2 teaspoon ginger paste
- 1/2 teaspoon garlic paste
- 1/2 teaspoon cumin seeds
- 1/2 teaspoon turmeric powder
- 1/2 teaspoon red chili powder
- 1/2 teaspoon coriander powder
- 1/2 teaspoon garam masala
- Salt to taste
- 1/2 cup chopped cilantro
- 1 cup water

Instructions:

1. In a large pan, heat the oil over medium heat.

2. Add the onion and cook until golden brown, about 5 minutes.

3. Add the ginger paste, garlic paste, cumin seeds, turmeric powder, red chili powder, coriander powder, garam masala, and salt to the pan. Cook until the spices are fragrant, about 5 minutes.

4. Stir in the climbing perch fish fillets and cook for an additional 5-7 minutes, or until the fish is cooked through.

5. Stir in the cilantro and cook for an additional 5 minutes.

6. Pour in the water and bring to a boil. Reduce heat to low and let the curry simmer for 10-15 minutes, or until the sauce has thickened slightly.

7. Serve the koi macher jhol hot over rice as a main dish.

SHRIMP MALAI CURRY
(SHRIMP IN COCONUT MILK)

Ingredients:

- 1 lb shrimp, peeled and deveined
- 2 tablespoons oil
- 1 onion, chopped
- 1/2 teaspoon ginger paste
- 1/2 teaspoon garlic paste
- 1/2 teaspoon cumin seeds
- 1/2 teaspoon turmeric powder
- 1/2 teaspoon red chili powder
- 1/2 teaspoon coriander powder
- 1/2 teaspoon garam masala
- Salt to taste
- 1 can coconut milk
- 1/2 cup chopped cilantro

Instructions:

1. In a large pan, heat the oil over medium heat.

2. Add the onion and cook until golden brown, about 5 minutes.

3. Add the ginger paste, garlic paste, cumin seeds, turmeric powder, red chili powder, coriander powder, garam masala, and salt to the pan. Cook until the spices are fragrant, about 5 minutes.

4. Stir in the shrimp and cook until they are pink and cooked through, about 5-7 minutes.

5. Stir in the coconut milk and bring to a boil. Reduce heat to low and let the sauce simmer for 10-15 minutes, or until the sauce has thickened slightly.

6. Stir in the cilantro and cook for an additional 5 minutes.

7. Serve the shrimp malai curry hot over rice as a main dish.

CHINGRI MACHER MALAIKARI (SHRIMP IN COCONUT SAUCE)

Ingredients:

- 1 lb shrimp, peeled and deveined
- 2 tablespoons oil
- 1 onion, chopped
- 1/2 teaspoon ginger paste
- 1/2 teaspoon garlic paste
- 1/2 teaspoon cumin seeds
- 1/2 teaspoon turmeric powder
- 1/2 teaspoon red chili powder
- 1/2 teaspoon coriander powder
- 1/2 teaspoon garam masala
- Salt to taste
- 1 can coconut milk
- 1/2 cup chopped cilantro

Instructions:

1. In a large pan, heat the oil over medium heat.

2. Add the onion and cook until golden brown, about 5 minutes.

3. Add the ginger paste, garlic paste, cumin seeds, turmeric powder, red chili powder, coriander powder, garam masala, and salt to the pan. Cook until the spices are fragrant, about 5 minutes.

4. Stir in the shrimp and cook until they are pink and cooked through, about 5-7 minutes.

5. Stir in the coconut milk and bring to a boil. Reduce heat to low and let the sauce simmer for 10-15 minutes, or until the sauce has thickened slightly.

6. Stir in the cilantro and cook for an additional 5 minutes.

7. Serve the chingri macher malaikari hot over rice as a main dish.

CHINGRI BHAPE (STEAMED SHRIMP)

Ingredients:

- 1 lb shrimp, peeled and deveined
- 2 tablespoons oil
- 1 onion, chopped
- 1/2 teaspoon ginger paste
- 1/2 teaspoon garlic paste
- 1/2 teaspoon turmeric powder
- 1/2 teaspoon red chili powder
- 1/2 teaspoon coriander powder
- 1/2 teaspoon garam masala
- Salt to taste
- 1/2 cup water
- 1/2 cup chopped cilantro

Instructions:

1. In a large pan, heat the oil over medium heat.

2. Add the onion and cook until golden brown, about 5 minutes.

3. Add the ginger paste, garlic paste, turmeric powder, red chili powder, coriander powder, garam masala, and salt to the pan. Cook until the spices are fragrant, about 5 minutes.

4. Stir in the shrimp and cook until they are pink and cooked through, about 5-7 minutes.

5. Pour in the water and bring to a boil. Reduce heat to low and let the sauce simmer for 10-15 minutes, or until the sauce has thickened slightly.

6. Stir in the cilantro and cook for an additional 5 minutes.

7. Serve the chingri bhape hot as a main dish or side dish.

LOITTA MACHER JHURI (BOMBAY DUCK FISH STIR-FRY)

Ingredients:

- 1 lb Bombay duck fish fillets, cut into pieces
- 2 tablespoons oil
- 1 onion, chopped
- 1/2 teaspoon ginger paste
- 1/2 teaspoon garlic paste
- 1/2 teaspoon turmeric powder
- 1/2 teaspoon red chili powder
- 1/2 teaspoon coriander powder
- 1/2 teaspoon garam masala
- Salt to taste
- 1/2 cup chopped cilantro

Instructions:

1. In a large pan, heat the oil over medium heat.

2. Add the onion and cook until golden brown, about 5 minutes.

3. Add the ginger paste, garlic paste, turmeric powder, red chili powder, coriander powder, garam masala, and salt to the pan. Cook until the spices are fragrant, about 5 minutes.

4. Stir in the Bombay duck fish and cook until they are browned on both sides, about 5-7 minutes.

5. Stir in the cilantro and cook for an additional 2-3 minutes.

6. Serve the loitta macher jhuri hot as a main dish or side dish.

CRAB KALIA (CRAB CURRY)

Ingredients:

- 1 lb crab, cleaned and cut into pieces
- 2 tablespoons oil
- 1 onion, chopped
- 1/2 teaspoon ginger paste
- 1/2 teaspoon garlic paste
- 1/2 teaspoon cumin seeds
- 1/2 teaspoon turmeric powder
- 1/2 teaspoon red chili powder
- 1/2 teaspoon coriander powder
- 1/2 teaspoon garam masala
- Salt to taste
- 1 cup water
- 1/2 cup chopped cilantro

Instructions:

1. In a large pan, heat the oil over medium heat.

2. Add the onion and cook until golden brown, about 5 minutes.

3. Add the ginger paste, garlic paste, cumin seeds, turmeric powder, red chili powder, coriander powder, garam masala, and salt to the pan. Cook until the spices are fragrant, about 5 minutes.

4. Stir in the crab and cook until they are browned on both sides, about 5-7 minutes.

5. Pour in the water and bring to a boil. Reduce heat to low and let the sauce simmer for 10-15 minutes, or until the sauce has thickened slightly.

6. Stir in the cilantro and cook for an additional 5 minutes.

7. Serve the crab kalia hot over rice as a main dish.

TILAPIA SHORSHE
(TILAPIA IN MUSTARD SAUCE)

Ingredients:

- 1 lb tilapia fillets
- 2 tablespoons oil
- 1 onion, chopped
- 1/2 teaspoon ginger paste
- 1/2 teaspoon garlic paste
- 1/2 teaspoon mustard seeds
- 1/2 teaspoon turmeric powder
- 1/2 teaspoon red chili powder
- 1/2 teaspoon coriander powder
- 1/2 teaspoon garam masala
- Salt to taste
- 1/2 cup mustard sauce
- 1/2 cup chopped cilantro

Instructions:

1. In a large pan, heat the oil over medium heat.

2. Add the onion and cook until golden brown, about 5 minutes.

3. Add the ginger paste, garlic paste, mustard seeds, turmeric powder, red chili powder, coriander powder, garam masala, and salt to the pan. Cook until the spices are fragrant, about 5 minutes.

4. Stir in the tilapia fillets and cook until they are browned on both sides, about 5-7 minutes.

5. Stir in the mustard sauce and bring to a boil. Reduce heat to low and let the sauce simmer for 10-15 minutes, or until the sauce has thickened slightly.

6. Stir in the cilantro and cook for an additional 2-3 minutes.

7. Serve the tilapia shorshe hot as a main dish or side dish.

RUPCHANDA MACHER JHOL (POMFRET FISH CURRY)

Ingredients:

- 1 lb pomfret fish fillets
- 2 tablespoons oil
- 1 onion, chopped
- 1/2 teaspoon ginger paste
- 1/2 teaspoon garlic paste
- 1/2 teaspoon cumin seeds
- 1/2 teaspoon turmeric powder
- 1/2 teaspoon red chili powder
- 1/2 teaspoon coriander powder

- 1/2 teaspoon garam masala
- Salt to taste
- 1 cup water
- 1/2 cup chopped cilantro

Instructions:

1. In a large pan, heat the oil over medium heat.

2. Add the onion and cook until golden brown, about 5 minutes.

3. Add the ginger paste, garlic paste, cumin seeds, turmeric powder, red chili powder, coriander powder, garam masala, and salt to the pan. Cook until the spices are fragrant, about 5 minutes.

4. Stir in the pomfret fish fillets and cook until they are browned on both sides, about 5-7 minutes.

5. Pour in the water and bring to a boil. Reduce heat to low and let the sauce simmer for 10-15 minutes, or until the sauce has thickened slightly.

6. Stir in the cilantro and cook for an additional 2-3 minutes.

7. Serve the rupchanda macher jhol hot over rice as a main dish.

MEATS

CHICKEN ROAST

Ingredients:

- 1 lb chicken, cut into pieces
- 2 tablespoons oil
- 1 onion, chopped
- 1/2 teaspoon ginger paste
- 1/2 teaspoon garlic paste
- 1/2 teaspoon turmeric powder
- 1/2 teaspoon red chili powder
- 1/2 teaspoon coriander powder
- 1/2 teaspoon garam masala
- Salt to taste
- 1/2 cup chopped cilantro

Instructions:

1. In a large pan, heat the oil over medium heat.

2. Add the onion and cook until golden brown, about 5 minutes.

3. Add the ginger paste, garlic paste, turmeric powder, red chili powder, coriander powder, garam masala, and salt to the pan. Cook until the spices are fragrant, about 5 minutes.

4. Stir in the chicken pieces and cook until they are browned on both sides, about 10-15 minutes.

5. Stir in the cilantro and cook for an additional 2-3 minutes.

6. Serve the chicken roast hot as a main dish or side dish.

MUTTON KORMA

Ingredients:

- 1 lb mutton, cut into pieces
- 2 tablespoons oil
- 1 onion, chopped
- 1/2 teaspoon ginger paste
- 1/2 teaspoon garlic paste
- 1/2 teaspoon turmeric powder
- 1/2 teaspoon red chili powder
- 1/2 teaspoon coriander powder
- 1/2 teaspoon garam masala
- Salt to taste
- 1/2 cup plain yogurt
- 1/2 cup chopped cilantro

Instructions:

1. In a large pan, heat the oil over medium heat.

2. Add the onion and cook until golden brown, about 5 minutes.

3. Add the ginger paste, garlic paste, turmeric powder, red chili powder, coriander powder, garam masala, and salt to the pan. Cook until the spices are fragrant, about 5 minutes.

4. Stir in the mutton pieces and cook until they are browned on both sides, about 10-15 minutes.

5. Stir in the yogurt and cook until the mutton is tender, about 10-15 minutes.

6. Stir in the cilantro and cook for an additional 2-3 minutes.

7. Serve the mutton korma hot over rice as a main dish.

BEEF KALA BHUNA

Ingredients:

- 1 lb beef, cut into pieces
- 2 tablespoons oil
- 1 onion, chopped
- 1/2 teaspoon ginger paste
- 1/2 teaspoon garlic paste
- 1/2 teaspoon turmeric powder
- 1/2 teaspoon red chili powder
- 1/2 teaspoon coriander powder
- 1/2 teaspoon garam masala
- Salt to taste
- 1/2 cup chopped cilantro

Instructions:

1. In a large pan, heat the oil over medium heat.

2. Add the onion and cook until golden brown, about 5 minutes.

3. Add the ginger paste, garlic paste, turmeric powder, red chili powder, coriander powder, garam masala, and salt to the pan. Cook until the spices are fragrant, about 5 minutes.

4. Stir in the beef pieces and cook until they are browned on both sides, about 10-15 minutes.

5. Stir in the cilantro and cook for an additional 2-3 minutes.

6. Serve the beef kala bhuna hot over rice as a main dish.

CHICKEN CHAAP

Ingredients:

- 1 lb chicken, cut into pieces
- 2 tablespoons oil
- 1 onion, chopped
- 1/2 teaspoon ginger paste
- 1/2 teaspoon garlic paste
- 1/2 teaspoon turmeric powder
- 1/2 teaspoon red chili powder
- 1/2 teaspoon coriander powder
- 1/2 teaspoon garam masala
- Salt to taste
- 1/2 cup chopped cilantro

Instructions:

1. In a large pan, heat the oil over medium heat.

2. Add the onion and cook until golden brown, about 5 minutes.

3. Add the ginger paste, garlic paste, turmeric powder, red chili powder, coriander powder, garam masala, and salt to the pan. Cook until the spices are fragrant, about 5 minutes.

4. Stir in the chicken pieces and cook until they are browned on both sides, about 10-15 minutes.

5. Stir in the cilantro and cook for an additional 2-3 minutes.

6. Serve the chicken chaap hot over rice as a main dish.

DUCK CURRY

Ingredients:

- 1 lb duck meat, cut into pieces
- 2 tablespoons oil
- 1 onion, chopped
- 1/2 teaspoon ginger paste
- 1/2 teaspoon garlic paste
- 1/2 teaspoon turmeric powder
- 1/2 teaspoon red chili powder
- 1/2 teaspoon coriander powder
- 1/2 teaspoon garam masala
- Salt to taste
- 1/2 cup chopped cilantro

Instructions:

1. In a large pan, heat the oil over medium heat.

2. Add the onion and cook until golden brown, about 5 minutes.

3. Add the ginger paste, garlic paste, turmeric powder, red chili powder, coriander powder, garam masala, and salt to the pan. Cook until the spices are fragrant, about 5 minutes.

4. Stir in the duck meat and cook until browned on both sides, about 10-15 minutes.

5. Stir in the cilantro and cook for an additional 2-3 minutes.

6. Serve the duck curry hot over rice as a main dish.

QUAIL CURRY

Ingredients:

- 1 lb quail
- 2 medium onions, chopped
- 3 cloves of garlic, minced
- 1 inch piece of ginger, minced
- 1 tbsp coriander powder
- 1 tsp cumin powder
- 1 tsp turmeric powder
- 1 tsp paprika
- 1 tsp garam masala
- 1 tsp salt
- 1 cup tomato puree
- 1 cup water
- 2 tbsp oil

Instructions:

1. In a large pan, heat the oil over medium heat. Add the onions, garlic, and ginger and cook until the onions are soft and translucent, about 5 minutes.

2. Add the coriander powder, cumin powder, turmeric powder, paprika, garam masala, and salt to the pan and cook for 1 minute.

3. Add the tomato puree and water to the pan and bring to a boil. Reduce heat to low and let the sauce simmer for 10 minutes.

4. Add the quail to the pan and cook until they are fully cooked, about 20-25 minutes.

5. Serve hot with rice or bread of your choice.

BEEF TEHARI

Ingredients:

- 1 lb beef, cut into 1-inch cubes
- 2 medium onions, chopped
- 3 cloves of garlic, minced
- 1 inch piece of ginger, minced
- 2 tbsp coriander powder
- 1 tsp cumin powder
- 1 tsp turmeric powder
- 1 tsp paprika
- 1 tsp garam masala
- 1 tsp salt
- 1 cup tomato puree
- 1 cup water
- 2 tbsp oil
- 1 cup basmati rice
- 2 cups water
- 1 tsp salt

Instructions:

1. In a large pan, heat the oil over medium heat. Add the onions, garlic, and ginger and cook until the onions are soft and translucent, about 5 minutes.

2. Add the coriander powder, cumin powder, turmeric powder, paprika, garam masala, and salt to the pan and cook for 1 minute.

3. Add the tomato puree and water to the pan and bring to a boil. Reduce heat to low and let the sauce simmer for 10 minutes.

4. Add the beef to the pan and cook until it is fully cooked, about 20-25 minutes.

5. While the beef is cooking, rinse the rice in cold water and drain. In a separate pot, bring 2 cups of water and 1 tsp of salt to a boil. Add the rice to the pot, reduce heat to low, and let it cook for 18-20 minutes, or until the water is fully absorbed and the rice is cooked through.

6. Serve the beef on top of a bed of cooked rice.

BREADS

LUCHI (DEEP-FRIED BREAD)

Ingredients:

- 2 cups all-purpose flour
- 1 tsp salt
- 2 tbsp ghee or oil
- Water as needed
- Oil for deep frying

Instructions:

1. In a large bowl, combine the flour, salt, ghee or oil, and enough water to form a soft dough.

2. Knead the dough for 5-7 minutes, or until it is smooth and elastic. Cover the dough with a damp cloth and let it rest for 15-20 minutes.

3. Divide the dough into 12 equal-sized balls. On a floured surface, roll each ball into a thin, round circle.

4. In a deep pot, heat the oil over medium heat. When the oil is hot, carefully place a rolled-out dough circle into the oil and cook until it is golden brown, about 2 minutes per side.

5. Repeat with the remaining dough balls.

6. Serve the luchi hot with your favorite curry or stew.

PARATHA (LAYERED FLATBREAD)

Ingredients:

- 2 cups all-purpose flour
- 1 tsp salt
- 2 tbsp ghee or oil
- Water as needed
- Oil for cooking

Instructions:

1. In a large bowl, combine the flour, salt, ghee or oil, and enough water to form a soft dough.

2. Knead the dough for 5-7 minutes, or until it is smooth and elastic. Cover the dough with a damp cloth and let it rest for 15-20 minutes.

3. Divide the dough into 8 equal-sized balls. On a floured surface, roll each ball into a thin, round circle.

4. Heat a large pan over medium heat. When the pan is hot, place a rolled-out dough circle onto the pan and cook for 1-2 minutes on each side, or until light brown spots start to appear.

5. Remove the dough from the pan and place it onto a plate. Using a rolling pin, gently flatten the dough, making sure to keep the edges thicker than the center.

6. Place 1 tsp of oil onto the center of the dough and spread it evenly over the surface, making sure to reach the edges. Fold the edges of the dough towards the center to form a ball.

7. Flatten the dough ball into a thin circle using a rolling pin. Repeat the process of cooking, flattening, and oiling the dough, until the dough has been layered and cooked at least 4-5 times.

8. Place the layered dough back onto the pan and cook until both sides are crispy and golden brown, about 2-3 minutes per side.

9. Serve the paratha hot with your favorite side dish or condiment.

NAAN (LEAVENED BREAD)

Ingredients:

- 2 cups all-purpose flour
- 1 tsp active dry yeast
- 1 tsp sugar
- 1 tsp salt
- 1/4 cup plain yogurt
- 1/4 cup warm water
- 2 tbsp ghee or melted butter
- Water as needed

Instructions:

1. In a large bowl, combine the flour, yeast, sugar, and salt. In a separate bowl, mix together the yogurt, warm water, and ghee or melted butter.

2. Pour the yogurt mixture into the dry ingredients and mix until a soft dough forms. If the dough is too dry, add water as needed, one tablespoon at a time.

3. Knead the dough for 5-7 minutes, or until it is smooth and elastic. Cover the dough with a damp cloth and let it rise in a warm place for 1-2 hours, or until doubled in size.

4. Preheat a cast iron pan or griddle over medium heat.

5. Divide the dough into 8 equal-sized balls. On a floured surface, roll each ball into a thin, oval shape.

6. Place the rolled-out dough onto the hot pan and cook for 1-2 minutes on each side, or until light brown spots start to appear and bubbles form on the surface of the dough.

7. Brush the cooked naan with melted butter or ghee, if desired.

8. Serve the naan hot with your favorite curry or stew.

KULCHA
(LEAVENED BREAD WITH STUFFING)

Ingredients:

- 2 cups all-purpose flour
- 1 tsp active dry yeast
- 1 tsp sugar
- 1 tsp salt
- 1/4 cup plain yogurt
- 1/4 cup warm water
- 2 tbsp ghee or melted butter
- Water as needed
- 1 cup finely chopped onion
- 1/2 cup finely chopped cilantro
- 1 tsp salt
- 1 tsp chaat masala

Instructions:

1. In a large bowl, combine the flour, yeast, sugar, and salt. In a separate bowl, mix together the yogurt, warm water, and ghee or melted butter.

2. Pour the yogurt mixture into the dry ingredients and mix until a soft dough forms. If the dough is too dry, add water as needed, one tablespoon at a time.

3. Knead the dough for 5-7 minutes, or until it is smooth and elastic. Cover the dough with a damp cloth and let it rise in a warm place for 1-2 hours, or until doubled in size.

4. In a small bowl, mix together the onion, cilantro, salt, and chaat masala to make the stuffing.

5. Divide the dough into 8 equal-sized balls. On a floured surface, roll each ball into a thin, round circle.

6. Place 2 tbsp of the stuffing mixture onto the center of each rolled-out dough circle. Gather the edges of the dough towards the center and pinch them together to form a ball, making sure the stuffing is fully enclosed inside the dough.

7. Roll the dough balls out into thin, round circles, making sure to keep the stuffing enclosed inside the dough.

8. Preheat a cast iron pan or griddle over medium heat.

9. Place the rolled-out dough onto the hot pan and cook for 2-3 minutes on each side, or until light brown spots start to appear and bubbles form on the surface of the dough.

10. Brush the cooked kulcha with melted butter or ghee, if desired.

11. Serve the kulcha hot with your favorite side dish or condiment.

ROTI (UNLEAVENED BREAD)

Ingredients:

- 2 cups whole wheat flour
- 1 tsp salt
- 2 tbsp ghee or oil

- Water as needed

Instructions:

1. In a large bowl, combine the flour, salt, and ghee or oil. Gradually add water and mix until a soft dough forms.

2. Knead the dough for 5-7 minutes, or until it is smooth and elastic. Cover the dough with a damp cloth and let it rest for 15-20 minutes.

3. Divide the dough into 8 equal-sized balls. On a floured surface, roll each ball into a thin, round circle.

4. Heat a large pan over medium heat. When the pan is hot, place a rolled-out dough circle onto the pan and cook for 1-2 minutes on each side, or until light brown spots start to appear.

5. Repeat with the remaining dough balls.

6. Serve the roti hot with your favorite curry or stew.

TANDOORI ROTI
(CLAY OVEN-BAKED BREAD)

Ingredients:

- 2 cups whole wheat flour
- 1 tsp salt
- 2 tbsp ghee or oil
- Water as needed

Instructions:

1. In a large bowl, combine the flour, salt, and ghee or oil. Gradually add water and mix until a soft dough forms.

2. Knead the dough for 5-7 minutes, or until it is smooth and elastic. Cover the dough with a damp cloth and let it rest for 15-20 minutes.

3. Divide the dough into 8 equal-sized balls. On a floured surface, roll each ball into a thin, round circle.

4. Preheat a tandoor or clay oven to high heat.

5. Place the rolled-out dough circles onto the hot walls of the tandoor or clay oven and cook for 2-3 minutes on each side, or until light brown spots start to appear and the roti puffs up.

6. Repeat with the remaining dough balls.

7. Serve the tandoori roti hot with your favorite curry or stew.

CHAPATI (THIN UNLEAVENED BREAD)

Ingredients:

- 2 cups whole wheat flour
- 1 tsp salt
- 2 tbsp ghee or oil
- Water as needed

Instructions:

1. In a large bowl, combine the flour, salt, and ghee or oil. Gradually add water and mix until a soft dough forms.

2. Knead the dough for 5-7 minutes, or until it is smooth and elastic. Cover the dough with a damp cloth and let it rest for 15-20 minutes.

3. Divide the dough into 8 equal-sized balls. On a floured surface, roll each ball into a thin, round circle.

4. Heat a large pan over medium heat. When the pan is hot, place a rolled-out dough circle onto the pan and cook for 1-2 minutes on each side, or until light brown spots start to appear.

5. Repeat with the remaining dough balls.

6. Serve the chapati hot with your favorite curry or stew.

TAFTAN
(LEAVENED BREAD WITH SAFFRON)

Ingredients:

- 2 cups all-purpose flour
- 1 tsp active dry yeast
- 1 tsp sugar
- 1 tsp salt
- 1/4 cup plain yogurt
- 1/4 cup warm water
- 2 tbsp ghee or melted butter
- Water as needed
- 1 tsp saffron threads
- 1 tsp milk

Instructions:

1. In a small bowl, soak the saffron threads in the milk for 5-10 minutes, or until the milk has turned a deep yellow color.

2. In a large bowl, combine the flour, yeast, sugar, and salt. In a separate bowl, mix together the yogurt, warm water, ghee or melted butter, and saffron milk mixture.

3. Pour the yogurt mixture into the dry ingredients and mix until a soft dough forms. If the dough is too dry, add water as needed, one tablespoon at a time.

4. Knead the dough for 5-7 minutes, or until it is smooth and elastic. Cover the dough with a damp cloth and let it rise in a warm place for 1-2 hours, or until doubled in size.

5. Preheat a cast iron pan or griddle over medium heat.

6. Divide the dough into 8 equal-sized balls. On a floured surface, roll each ball into a thin, oval shape.

7. Place the rolled-out dough onto the hot pan and cook for 1-2 minutes on each side, or until light brown spots start to appear and bubbles form on the surface of the dough.

8. Brush the cooked taftan with melted butter or ghee, if desired.

9. Serve the taftan hot with your favorite curry or stew.

PURI (DEEP-FRIED PUFFED BREAD)

Ingredients:

- 2 cups all-purpose flour
- 1 tsp salt
- 2 tbsp ghee or oil
- Water as needed
- Vegetable oil for deep-frying

Instructions:

1. In a large bowl, combine the flour, salt, and ghee or oil. Gradually add water and mix until a soft dough forms.

2. Knead the dough for 5-7 minutes, or until it is smooth and elastic. Cover the dough with a damp cloth and let it rest for 15-20 minutes.

3. Divide the dough into 8 equal-sized balls. On a floured surface, roll each ball into a thin, round circle.

4. Heat the vegetable oil in a large, deep saucepan over medium-high heat. The oil should be deep enough so that the puri can float freely and puff up.

5. Carefully place a rolled-out dough circle into the hot oil. As soon as it touches the oil, it should start to puff up.

6. Fry the puri for 1-2 minutes on each side, or until it is golden brown and fully puffed up.

7. Repeat with the remaining dough balls.

8. Serve the puri hot with your favorite curry or stew.

BAKARKHANI (SWEET FLAKY BREAD)

Ingredients:

- 2 cups all-purpose flour
- 1 tsp active dry yeast
- 1 tsp sugar
- 1 tsp salt
- 1/4 cup plain yogurt
- 1/4 cup warm water
- 2 tbsp ghee or melted butter
- Water as needed
- 1 tsp cardamom powder
- 1 tsp sugar

Instructions:

1. In a large bowl, combine the flour, yeast, sugar, and salt. In a separate bowl, mix together the yogurt, warm water, and ghee or melted butter.

2. Pour the yogurt mixture into the dry ingredients and mix until a soft dough forms. If the dough is too dry, add water as needed, one tablespoon at a time.

3. Knead the dough for 5-7 minutes, or until it is smooth and elastic. Cover the dough with a damp cloth and let it rise in a warm place for 1-2 hours, or until doubled in size.

4. In a small bowl, mix together the cardamom powder and sugar.

5. Preheat the oven to 375°F (190°C). Line a baking sheet with parchment paper.

6. Divide the dough into 8 equal-sized balls. On a floured surface, roll each ball into a thin, round circle.

7. Brush the rolled-out dough circles with melted ghee or butter and sprinkle with the cardamom sugar mixture.

8. Place the bakarkhani onto the prepared baking sheet and bake for 15-20 minutes, or until the bread is golden brown and crispy.

9. Serve the bakarkhani warm or at room temperature.

SHEERMAL
(SWEET SAFFRON-FLAVORED BREAD)

Ingredients:

- 2 cups all-purpose flour
- 1 tsp active dry yeast
- 1 tsp sugar
- 1 tsp salt
- 1/4 cup plain yogurt
- 1/4 cup warm water

- 2 tbsp ghee or melted butter
- Water as needed
- 1 tsp saffron threads
- 1 tsp milk
- 1 tsp sugar

Instructions:

1. In a small bowl, soak the saffron threads in the milk for 5-10 minutes, or until the milk has turned a deep yellow color.

2. In a large bowl, combine the flour, yeast, sugar, and salt. In a separate bowl, mix together the yogurt, warm water, ghee or melted butter, and saffron milk mixture.

3. Pour the yogurt mixture into the dry ingredients and mix until a soft dough forms. If the dough is too dry, add water as needed, one tablespoon at a time.

4. Knead the dough for 5-7 minutes, or until it is smooth and elastic. Cover the dough with a damp cloth and let it rise in a warm place for 1-2 hours, or until doubled in size.

5. Preheat the oven to 375°F (190°C). Line a baking sheet with parchment paper.

6. Divide the dough into 8 equal-sized balls. On a floured surface, roll each ball into a thin, round circle.

7. Brush the rolled-out dough circles with melted ghee or butter and sprinkle with the sugar.

8. Place the sheermal onto the prepared baking sheet and bake for 15-20 minutes, or until the bread is golden brown and crispy.

9. Serve the sheermal warm or at room temperature.

BEVERAGES

BORHANI (SPICED YOGURT DRINK)

Ingredients:

- 2 cups plain yogurt
- 1/2 cup water
- 1/4 cup mint leaves
- 1/4 cup cilantro leaves
- 1 jalapeno pepper, seeded and chopped
- 1 garlic clove, minced
- 1 tsp salt
- 1 tsp cumin powder
- 1 tsp sugar
- 1 tsp black salt

Instructions:

1. In a blender, combine the yogurt, water, mint leaves, cilantro leaves, jalapeno pepper, garlic, salt, cumin powder, sugar, and black salt.

2. Blend until the mixture is smooth and well combined.

3. Pour the borhani into glasses and serve chilled.

LASSI (YOGURT-BASED DRINK)

Ingredients:

- 2 cups plain yogurt
- 1/2 cup water
- 1/4 cup sugar
- 1 tsp cardamom powder
- 1 tsp rose water
- Ice cubes

Instructions:

1. In a blender, combine the yogurt, water, sugar, cardamom powder, and rose water.

2. Blend until the mixture is smooth and well combined.

3. Pour the lassi into glasses and add ice cubes. Serve chilled.

CHAAS (SPICED BUTTERMILK)

Ingredients:

- 2 cups plain yogurt
- 1/2 cup water
- 1 tsp cumin powder
- 1 tsp salt
- 1 tsp sugar
- 1/4 tsp black pepper
- 1/4 cup chopped cilantro
- Ice cubes

Instructions:

1. In a blender, combine the yogurt, water, cumin powder, salt, sugar, black pepper, and cilantro.

2. Blend until the mixture is smooth and well combined.

3. Pour the chaas into glasses and add ice cubes. Serve chilled.

GHOL (SWEET YOGURT DRINK)

Ingredients:

- 2 cups plain yogurt
- 1/2 cup water
- 1/4 cup sugar
- 1 tsp cardamom powder
- 1 tsp rose water
- Ice cubes

Instructions:

1. In a blender, combine the yogurt, water, sugar, cardamom powder, and rose water.

2. Blend until the mixture is smooth and well combined.

3. Pour the ghol into glasses and add ice cubes. Serve chilled.

AAM PANNA (RAW MANGO DRINK)

Ingredients:

- 2 raw mangoes, peeled and chopped
- 1/2 cup sugar
- 1 tsp cumin powder
- 1 tsp salt
- 1/2 tsp black salt
- 1/2 tsp roasted cumin powder
- 1/2 cup water

- Ice cubes

Instructions:

1. In a blender, combine the mangoes, sugar, cumin powder, salt, black salt, roasted cumin powder, and water.

2. Blend until the mixture is smooth and well combined.

3 . Strain the mixture through a fine mesh strainer to remove any fibers or seeds.

4. Pour the aam panna into glasses and add ice cubes. Serve chilled.

LEBUR SHARBAT (LEMONADE)

Ingredients:

- 1 cup freshly squeezed lemon juice
- 1 cup sugar
- 4 cups water
- Ice cubes

Instructions:

1. In a large pitcher, mix together the lemon juice, sugar, and water until the sugar is dissolved.

2. Pour the lebur sharbat into glasses and add ice cubes. Serve chilled.

TAMARIND SHARBAT
(TAMARIND DRINK)

Ingredients:

- 1 cup tamarind paste
- 1 cup sugar
- 4 cups water
- Ice cubes

Instructions:

1. In a large pitcher, mix together the tamarind paste, sugar, and water until the sugar is dissolved.

2. Strain the mixture through a fine mesh strainer to remove any fibers or seeds.

3. Pour the tamarind sharbat into glasses and add ice cubes. Serve chilled.

FALOODA
(MILK AND ROSE SYRUP DESSERT DRINK)

Ingredients:

- 2 cups milk
- 1/2 cup rose syrup
- 1/2 cup falooda noodles
- 1/4 cup basil seeds
- 1/4 cup chopped mixed fruit (such as mango, strawberry, and cherry)
- Ice cubes

Instructions:

1. In a large pitcher, mix together the milk and rose syrup.

2. Soak the falooda noodles and basil seeds in warm water for 15 minutes until they are soft and have swollen.

3. Divide the soaked noodles and basil seeds between 4 glasses.

4. Pour the milk and rose syrup mixture over the noodles and basil seeds in each glass.

5. Add a scoop of chopped mixed fruit on top of each glass.

6. Add ice cubes and serve immediately.

DUDH SHORBOT
(MILK AND ROSE SYRUP DRINK)

Ingredients:

- 2 cups milk
- 1/2 cup rose syrup
- 1 tsp cardamom powder
- Ice cubes

Instructions:

1. In a large pitcher, mix together the milk, rose syrup, and cardamom powder.

2. Pour the dudh shorbot into glasses and add ice cubes. Serve chilled.

PICKLES & CHUTNEYS

AAM ACHAR (MANGO PICKLE)

Ingredients:

- 5 ripe mangoes, peeled and chopped
- 1 cup mustard oil
- 1/2 cup mustard seeds
- 1/2 cup fenugreek seeds
- 1/2 cup cumin seeds
- 1/2 cup coriander seeds
- 1/2 cup fennel seeds
- 1 tsp turmeric powder
- 1 tsp red chili powder
- 1 tsp salt
- 1/2 tsp sugar

Instructions:

1. In a large saucepan, heat the mustard oil over medium heat until hot.

2. Add the mustard seeds, fenugreek seeds, cumin seeds, coriander seeds, and fennel seeds and cook for 2-3 minutes until fragrant.

3. Add the chopped mangoes, turmeric powder, red chili powder, salt, and sugar to the pan and stir to combine.

4. Reduce the heat to low and cook for 10-15 minutes until the mangoes are soft and the mixture is well combined.

5. Allow the aam achar to cool to room temperature and transfer to a sterilized glass jar. Store in the refrigerator for up to 1 month.

MIXED VEGETABLE ACHAR

Ingredients:

- 1 cup mixed vegetables (such as carrots, turnips, and green beans), chopped
- 1 cup mustard oil
- 1/2 cup mustard seeds
- 1/2 cup fenugreek seeds
- 1/2 cup c umin seeds
- 1/2 cup coriander seeds
- 1/2 cup fennel seeds
- 1 tsp turmeric powder
- 1 tsp red chili powder
- 1 tsp salt
- 1/2 tsp sugar

Instructions:

1. In a large saucepan, heat the mustard oil over medium heat until hot.

2. Add the mustard seeds, fenugreek seeds, cumin seeds, coriander seeds, and fennel seeds and cook for 2-3 minutes until fragrant.

3. Add the chopped mixed vegetables, turmeric powder, red chili powder, salt, and sugar to the pan and stir to combine.

4. Reduce the heat to low and cook for 10-15 minutes until the vegetables are soft and the mixture is well combined.

5. Allow the mixed vegetable achar to cool to room temperature and transfer to a sterilized glass jar. Store in the refrigerator for up to 1 month.

LIME PICKLE

Ingredients:

- 10 limes, chopped
- 1 cup mustard oil
- 1/2 cup mustard seeds
- 1/2 cup fenugreek seeds
- 1/2 cup cumin seeds
- 1/2 cup coriander seeds
- 1/2 cup fennel seeds
- 1 tsp turmeric powder
- 1 tsp red chili powder
- 1 tsp salt
- 1/2 tsp sugar

Instructions:

1. In a large saucepan, heat the mustard oil over medium heat until hot.

2. Add the mustard seeds, fenugreek seeds, cumin seeds, coriander seeds, and fennel seeds and cook for 2-3 minutes until fragrant.

3. Add the chopped limes, turmeric powder, red chili powder, salt, and sugar to the pan and stir to combine.

4. Reduce the heat to low and cook for 10-15 minutes until the limes are soft and the mixture is well combined.

5. Allow the lime pickle to cool to room temperature and transfer to a sterilized glass jar. Store in the refrigerator for up to 1 month.

TOMATO CHUTNEY

Ingredients:

- 5 ripe tomatoes, chopped
- 1/2 cup onion, chopped
- 2 cloves garlic, minced
- 1 inch ginger, minced
- 1 tsp red chili powder
- 1 tsp coriander powder
- 1 tsp cumin powder
- 1 tsp salt
- 1/2 tsp sugar
- 1/4 cup water
- 2 tbsp lemon juice

Instructions:

1. In a large saucepan, heat 1 tablespoon of oil over medium heat.

2. Add the onion, garlic, and ginger and cook for 2-3 minutes until fragrant.

3. Add the chopped tomatoes, red chili powder, coriander powder, cumin powder, salt, and sugar to the pan and stir to combine.

4. Pour in the water and lemon juice and stir to combine.

5. Reduce the heat to low and cook for 10-15 minutes until the tomatoes are soft and the mixture is well combined.

6. Allow the tomato chutney to cool to room temperature and transfer to a sterilized glass jar. Store in the refrigerator for up to 1 month.

GREEN MANGO CHUTNEY

Ingredients:

- 5 green mangoes, peeled and chopped
- 1/2 cup onion, chopped
- 2 cloves garlic, minced
- 1 inch ginger, minced
- 1 tsp red chili powder
- 1 tsp coriander powder
- 1 tsp cumin powder
- 1 tsp salt
- 1/2 tsp sugar
- 1/4 cup water
- 2 tbsp lemon juice

Instructions:

1. In a large saucepan, heat 1 tablespoon of oil over medium heat.

2. Add the onion, garlic, and ginger and cook for 2-3 minutes until fragrant.

3. Add the chopped green mangoes, red chili powder, coriander powder, cumin powder, salt, and sugar to the pan and stir to combine.

4. Pour in the water and lemon juice and stir to combine.

5. Reduce the heat to low and cook for 10-15 minutes until the mangoes are soft and the mixture is well combined.

6. Allow the green mango chutney to cool to room temperature and transfer to a sterilized glass jar. Store in the refrigerator for up to 1 month.

TAMARIND CHUTNEY

Ingredients:

- 1 cup tamarind paste
- 1/2 cup onion, chopped
- 2 cloves garlic, minced
- 1 inch ginger, minced
- 1 tsp red chili powder
- 1 tsp coriander powder
- 1 tsp cumin powder
- 1 tsp salt
- 1/2 tsp sugar
- 1/4 cup water

Instructions:

1. In a large saucepan, heat 1 tablespoon of oil over medium heat.

2. Add the onion, garlic, and ginger and cook for 2-3 minutes until fragrant.

3. Add the tamarind paste, red chili powder, coriander powder, cumin powder, salt, and sugar to the pan and stir to combine.

4. Pour in the water and stir to combine.

5. Reduce the heat to low and cook for 10-15 minutes until the mixture is well combined and has thickened slightly.

6. Allow the tamarind chutney to cool to room temperature and transfer to a sterilized glass jar. Store in the refrigerator for up to 1 month.

CORIANDER CHUTNEY

Ingredients:

- 1 cup fresh coriander, chopped
- 1/2 cup onion, chopped
- 2 cloves garlic, minced
- 1 inch ginger, minced
- 1 tsp green chili, chopped
- 1 tsp salt
- 1/2 tsp sugar
- 1/4 cup water
- 2 tbsp lemon juice

Instructions:

1. In a blender or food processor, combine the coriander, onion, garlic, ginger, green chili, salt, sugar, water, and lemon juice.

2. Blend until smooth and transfer to a sterilized glass jar. Store in the refrigerator for up to 1 week.

MINT CHUTNEY

Ingredients:

- 1 cup fresh mint leaves, chopped
- 1/2 cup onion, chopped
- 2 cloves garlic, minced
- 1 inch ginger, minced
- 1 tsp green chili, chopped
- 1 tsp salt
- 1/2 tsp sugar
- 1/4 cup water
- 2 tbsp lemon juice

Instructions:

1. In a blender or food processor, combine the mint leaves, onion, garlic, ginger, green chili, salt, sugar, water, and lemon juice.

2. Blend until smooth and transfer to a sterilized glass jar. Store in the refrigerator for up to 1 week.

SALADS

KACHUMBER SALAD

Ingredients:

- 2 large tomatoes, chopped
- 1 cucumber, chopped
- 1 onion, chopped
- 1 tsp salt
- 1 tsp sugar
- 2 tbsp lemon juice

Instructions:

1. In a large bowl, combine the chopped tomatoes, cucumber, and onion.

2. Add the salt, sugar, and lemon juice to the bowl and stir to combine.

3. Serve the kachumber salad immediately or refrigerate until ready to serve.

CUCUMBER RAITA

Ingredients:

- 2 cups plain yogurt
- 1 cucumber, grated
- 1 tsp salt

- 1/2 tsp sugar
- 2 tbsp mint leaves, chopped

Instructions:

1. In a large bowl, combine the yogurt, grated cucumber, salt, sugar, and chopped mint leaves.

2. Stir until well combined and refrigerate until ready to serve.

TOMATO AND ONION SALAD

Ingredients:

- 3 large tomatoes, chopped
- 1 onion, chopped
- 1 tsp salt
- 1 tsp sugar
- 2 tbsp lemon juice

Instructions:

1. In a large bowl, combine the chopped tomatoes and onion.

2. Add the salt, sugar, and lemon juice to the bowl and stir to combine.

3. Serve the tomato and onion salad immediately or refrigerate until ready to serve.

CHICKPEA SALAD

Ingredients:

- 2 cups chickpeas, cooked and drained

- 1 large tomato, chopped
- 1 onion, chopped
- 1 tsp salt
- 1 tsp sugar
- 2 tbsp lemon juice
- 2 tbsp cilantro, chopped

Instructions:

1. In a large bowl, combine the cooked chickpeas, chopped tomato, and onion.

2. Add the salt, sugar, lemon juice, and chopped cilantro to the bowl and stir to combine.

3. Serve the chickpea salad immediately or refrigerate until ready to serve.

SOUPS

MULLIGATAWNY SOUP

Ingredients:

- 1 tbsp vegetable oil
- 1 onion, chopped
- 2 cloves garlic, minced
- 1 inch ginger, minced
- 2 tsp ground cumin
- 2 tsp ground coriander
- 1 tsp turmeric
- 1 tsp red chili powder
- 1 tsp salt
- 4 cups chicken or vegetable broth
- 1 cup diced carrots
- 1 cup diced potatoes
- 1 cup diced tomatoes
- 1 cup cooked lentils
- 1/2 cup heavy cream (optional)

Instructions:

1. In a large pot, heat the oil over medium heat.

2. Add the onion, garlic, and ginger and cook for 2-3 minutes until fragrant.

3. Add the cumin, coriander, turmeric, red chili powder, and salt to the pot and stir to combine.

4. Pour in the broth, diced carrots, potatoes, tomatoes, and cooked lentils and stir to combine.

5. Bring the soup to a boil, then reduce the heat to low and let simmer for 20-30 minutes until the vegetables are tender.

6. If desired, stir in the heavy cream and let simmer for an additional 2-3 minutes.

7. Serve the mulligatawny soup hot, garnished with cilantro or other herbs if desired.

LENTIL SOUP

Ingredients:

- 1 tbsp vegetable oil
- 1 onion, chopped
- 2 cloves garlic, minced
- 1 inch ginger, minced
- 1 tsp ground cumin
- 1 tsp ground coriander
- 1 tsp turmeric
- 1 tsp salt
- 4 cups vegetable broth
- 1 cup red lentils, rinsed and drained
- 1 cup diced tomatoes
- 1/2 cup heavy cream (optional)

Instructions:

1. In a large pot, heat the oil over medium heat.

2. Add the onion, garlic, and ginger and cook for 2-3 minutes until fragrant.

3. Add the cumin, coriander, turmeric, and salt to the pot and stir to combine.

4. Pour in the vegetable broth, lentils, diced tomatoes, and stir to combine.

5. Bring the soup to a boil, then reduce the heat to low and let simmer for 20-30 minutes until the lentils are soft and tender.

6. If desired, stir in the heavy cream and let simmer for an additional 2-3 minutes.

7. Serve the lentil soup hot, garnished with cilantro or other herbs if desired.

VEGETABLE SOUP

Ingredients:

- 1 tbsp vegetable oil
- 1 onion, chopped
- 2 cloves garlic, minced
- 1 inch ginger, minced
- 2 carrots, chopped
- 2 potatoes, chopped
- 1 cup chopped green beans
- 1 cup corn kernels
- 1 tsp salt
- 4 cups vegetable broth
- 1 cup diced tomatoes
- 1/2 cup heavy cream (optional)

Instructions:

1. In a large pot, heat the oil over medium heat.

2. Add the onion, garlic, and ginger and cook for 2-3 minutes until fragrant.

3. Add the chopped carrots, potatoes, green beans, corn kernels, and salt to the pot and stir to combine.

4. Pour in the vegetable broth and diced tomatoes and stir to combine.

5. Bring the soup to a boil, then reduce the heat to low and let simmer for 20-30 minutes until the vegetables are tender.

6. If desired, stir in the heavy cream and let simmer for an additional 2-3 minutes.

7. Serve the vegetable soup hot, garnished with cilantro or other herbs if desired.

CHICKEN SOUP

Ingredients:

- 1 tbsp vegetable oil
- 1 onion, chopped
- 2 cloves garlic, minced
- 1 inch ginger, minced
- 2 carrots, chopped
- 2 potatoes, chopped
- 1 lb boneless, skinless chicken breast, cubed
- 1 tsp salt
- 4 cups chicken broth
- 1 cup diced tomatoes
- 1/2 cup heavy cream (optional)

Instructions:

1. In a large pot, heat the oil over medium heat.

2. Add the onion, garlic, and ginger and cook for 2-3 minutes until fragrant.

3. Add the chopped carrots, potatoes, cubed chicken, and salt to the pot and stir to combine.

4. Pour in the chicken broth and diced tomatoes and stir to combine.

5. Bring the soup to a boil, then reduce the heat to low and let simmer for 20-30 minutes until the chicken is cooked through and the vegetables are tender.

6. If desired, stir in the heavy cream and let simmer for an additional 2-3 minutes.

7. Serve the chicken soup hot, garnished with cilantro or other herbs if desired.

MUTTON SOUP

Ingredients:

- 1 tbsp vegetable oil
- 1 onion, chopped
- 2 cloves garlic, minced
- 1 inch ginger, minced
- 2 carrots, chopped
- 2 potatoes, chopped
- 1 lb boneless mutton, cubed
- 1 tsp salt
- 4 cups chicken broth
- 1 cup diced tomatoes
- 1/2 cup heavy cream (optional)

Instructions:

1. In a large pot, heat the oil over medium heat.

2. Add the onion, garlic, and ginger and cook for 2-3 minutes until fragrant.

3. Add the chopped carrots, potatoes, cubed mutton, and salt to the pot and stir to combine.

4. Pour in the chicken broth and diced tomatoes and stir to combine.

5. Bring the soup to a boil, then reduce the heat to low and let simmer for 30-40 minutes until the mutton is tender and fully cooked.

6. If desired, stir in the heavy cream and let simmer for an additional 2-3 minutes.

7. Serve the mutton soup hot, garnished with cilantro or other herbs if desired.

FISH SOUP

Ingredients:

- 1 tbsp vegetable oil
- 1 onion, chopped
- 2 cloves garlic, minced
- 1 inch ginger, minced
- 2 carrots, chopped
- 2 potatoes, chopped
- 1 lb fish fillets, cubed
- 1 tsp salt
- 4 cups fish broth or chicken broth
- 1 cup diced tomatoes
- 1/2 cup heavy cream (optional)

Instructions:

1. In a large pot, heat the oil over medium heat.

2. Add the onion, garlic, and ginger and cook for 2-3 minutes until fragrant.

3. Add the chopped carrots, potatoes, cubed fish, and salt to the pot and stir to combine.

4. Pour in the fish broth or chicken broth and diced tomatoes and stir to combine.

5. Bring the soup to a boil, then reduce the heat to low and let simmer for 10-15 minutes until the fish is fully cooked and the vegetables are tender.

6. If desired, stir in the heavy cream and let simmer for an additional 2-3 minutes.

7. Serve the fish soup hot, garnished with cilantro or other herbs if desired.

SHRIMP SOUP

Ingredients:

- 1 tbsp vegetable oil
- 1 onion, chopped
- 2 cloves garlic, minced
- 1 inch ginger, minced
- 2 carrots, chopped
- 2 potatoes, chopped
- 1 lb large shrimp, peeled and deveined
- 1 tsp salt
- 4 cups fish broth or chicken broth
- 1 cup diced tomatoes
- 1/2 cup heavy cream (optional)

Instructions:

1. In a large pot, heat the oil over medium heat.

2. Add the onion, garlic, and ginger and cook for 2-3 minutes until fragrant.

3. Add the chopped carrots, potatoes, shrimp, and salt to the pot and stir to combine.

4. Pour in the fish broth or chicken broth and diced tomatoes and stir to combine.

5. Bring the soup to a boil, then reduce the heat to low and let simmer for 5-7 minutes until the shrimp is fully cooked and the vegetables are tender.

6. If desired, stir in the heavy cream and let simmer for an additional 2-3 minutes.

7. Serve the shrimp soup hot, garnished with cilantro or other herbs if desired.

SIDES

PAPADUM (CRISPY LENTIL WAFERS)

Ingredients:

- 1 cup urad dal (split black lentils)
- 1 tsp salt
- 1 tsp cumin seeds
- 1 tsp black pepper
- 1 tsp red chili powder
- 1 tsp baking powder
- Vegetable oil for frying

Instructions:

1. Rinse and soak the urad dal in water for 4-5 hours.

2. Drain the water and grind the urad dal into a fine paste using a food processor or blender.

3. Mix in the salt, cumin seeds, black pepper, red chili powder, and baking powder into the urad dal paste and stir to combine.

4. Divide the mixture into 12-15 equal portions and shape each portion into a thin, round wafer.

5. Heat the vegetable oil in a large frying pan over medium heat.

6. Fry the papadum wafers in the hot oil for 1-2 minutes on each side until golden brown and crispy.

7. Remove the papadum from the oil and drain on a paper towel-lined plate.

8. Serve the papadum wafers hot with chutney or other dips of your choice.

BHORTA (MASHED VEGETABLES)

Ingredients:

- 2 large eggplants (aubergines)
- 2 large potatoes
- 2 large ripe tomatoes
- 1 small onion, chopped
- 2 cloves garlic, minced
- 1 inch ginger, minced
- 1 tsp salt
- 1 tsp cumin seeds
- 1 tsp coriander powder
- 1 tsp red chili powder
- 1 tsp turmeric powder
- 1 tbsp vegetable oil
- Fresh cilantro for garnish

Instructions:

1. Wash and peel the eggplants and potatoes, and chop them into small cubes.

2. Wash and chop the tomatoes into small pieces.

3. In a large pot, heat the oil over medium heat.

4. Add the chopped onion, garlic, and ginger and cook for 2-3 minutes until fragrant.

5. Add the chopped eggplants, potatoes, tomatoes, salt, cumin seeds, coriander powder, red chili powder, and turmeric powder to the pot and stir to combine.

6. Cover the pot and let cook for 10-15 minutes until the vegetables are soft and tender.

7. Mash the cooked vegetables using a potato masher or immersion blender until smooth.

8. Serve the bhorta hot, garnished with fresh cilantro.

RAITA (YOGURT-BASED SIDE DISH)

Ingredients:

- 2 cups plain yogurt
- 1 cucumber, peeled and grated
- 1 small onion, chopped
- 2 tbsp fresh mint, chopped
- 1 tsp salt
- 1 tsp cumin powder
- 1 tsp black pepper

Instructions:

1. In a large mixing bowl, whisk the yogurt until smooth and creamy.

2. Add the grated cucumber, chopped onion, fresh mint, salt, cumin powder, and black pepper to the bowl and stir to combine.

3. Chill the raita in the refrigerator for 30 minutes to an hour before serving.

4. Serve the raita as a side dish with rice, roti, or any Indian dish of your choice.

FRIED PLANTAINS

1. Slice the plantains into 1/2-inch rounds.

2. Heat the vegetable oil in a large frying pan over medium heat.

3. Fry the plantain slices in the hot oil for 2-3 minutes on each side until golden brown and crispy.

4. Remove the fried plantains from the oil and drain on a paper towel-lined plate.

5. Serve the fried plantains hot as a side dish or snack.

BRINJAL FRY (EGGPLANT FRY)

Ingredients:

- 2 large eggplants (aubergines)
- 1 cup all-purpose flour
- 1 tsp salt
- 1 tsp red chili powder
- 1 tsp turmeric powder
- 1 tsp coriander powder
- 1 tsp cumin powder
- Vegetable oil for frying

Instructions:

1. Wash and slice the eggplants into 1/2-inch rounds.

2. In a large mixing bowl, mix together the all-purpose flour, salt, red chili powder, turmeric powder, coriander powder, and cumin powder.

3. Dip each eggplant slice into the flour mixture, making sure it is fully coated.

4. Heat the vegetable oil in a large frying pan over medium heat.

5. Fry the coated eggplant slices in the hot oil for 2-3 minutes on each side until golden brown and crispy.

6. Remove the fried eggplants from the oil and drain on a paper towel-lined plate.

7. Serve the brinjal fry hot as a side dish or snack.

STREET FOOD

JHAL MURI (SPICY PUFFED RICE)

Ingredients:

- 4 cups puffed rice
- 1 small onion, chopped
- 2 tbsp chopped fresh cilantro
- 1 large tomato, chopped
- 1 green chili, chopped
- 1 tsp salt
- 1 tsp red chili powder
- 1 tsp chaat masala
- 1 tsp roasted cumin powder
- 2 tbsp lemon juice

Instructions:

1. In a large mixing bowl, mix together the puffed rice, chopped onion, chopped cilantro, chopped tomato, chopped green chili, salt, red chili powder, chaat masala, roasted cumin powder, and lemon juice.

2 / 2

2. Toss the ingredients together until well combined and the spices are evenly distributed.

3. Serve the jhal muri immediately, garnished with additional chopped cilantro and a squeeze of lemon juice, if desired.

FUCHKA (PANIPURI)

Ingredients:

- 1 cup all-purpose flour
- 1/2 cup semolina
- 1 tsp salt
- 1 tsp sugar
- 1 tbsp vegetable oil
- Water, as needed
- Vegetable oil for deep-frying
- 1 cup boiled and mashed potatoes
- 1/2 cup chickpeas, boiled
- 1 small onion, finely chopped
- 2 tbsp chopped cilantro
- 1 tsp red chili powder
- 1 tsp chaat masala
- 1 tsp roasted cumin powder
- 1 tsp tamarind chutney
- 1 tsp green mint chutney
- Lemon juice, to taste

Instructions:

1. In a large mixing bowl, mix together the all-purpose flour, semolina, salt, sugar, vegetable oil, and water to form a soft dough.

2. Cover the dough and let rest for 15-20 minutes.

3. Divide the dough into small balls and roll each ball into a thin circle.

4. Heat the vegetable oil for deep-frying in a large pot over medium heat.

5. Fry the rolled dough circles in the hot oil until puffed and golden brown, about 1-2 minutes on each side.

6. Remove the fried dough circles and drain on a paper towel-lined plate.

7. To assemble the fuchka, make a small hole in the center of each fried dough circle and fill with the mashed potatoes, boiled chickpeas, chopped onion, chopped cilantro, red chili powder, chaat masala, roasted cumin powder, tamarind chutney, green mint chutney, and lemon juice to taste.

8. Serve the fuchka immediately, garnished with additional chopped cilantro and a squeeze of lemon juice, if desired.

GHUGNI (SPICY YELLOW PEAS)

Ingredients:

- 2 cups dried yellow peas, soaked overnight
- 1 onion, chopped
- 1 large tomato, chopped
- 2 cloves garlic, minced
- 1 inch ginger, grated
- 1 green chili, chopped
- 1 tsp salt
- 1 tsp red chili powder
- 1 tsp turmeric powder
- 1 tsp coriander powder
- 1 tsp cumin powder
- 2 tbsp chopped cilantro
- 1 tbsp lemon juice

Instructions:

1. Boil the soaked yellow peas in a large pot of water until tender, about 25-30 minutes.

2. Drain the boiled yellow peas and set aside.

3. Heat a large saucepan over medium heat and add the chopped onion, chopped tomato, minced garlic, grated ginger, and chopped green chili.

4. Cook the mixture until the onion is translucent, about 5-7 minutes.

5. Add the cooked yellow peas to the saucepan and stir to combine.

6. Add the salt, red chili powder, turmeric powder, coriander powder, and cumin powder to the saucepan and stir to combine.

7. Cook the ghugni for an additional 5-7 minutes, until the flavors have melded and the mixture is heated through.

8. Stir in the chopped cilantro and lemon juice, and serve hot as a snack or side dish.

ALOO KABLI (SPICY POTATO SALAD)

Ingredients:

- 4 large potatoes, peeled and diced
- 1 onion, chopped
- 1 large tomato, chopped
- 2 tbsp chopped cilantro
- 1 green chili, chopped
- 1 tsp salt
- 1 tsp red chili powder
- 1 tsp cumin powder
- 1 tsp coriander powder
- 1 tsp chaat masala
- 1 tbsp lemon juice

Instructions:

1. Boil the diced potatoes in a large pot of water until tender, about 15-20 minutes.

2. Drain the boiled potatoes and set aside to cool slightly.

3. In a large mixing bowl, mix together the cooked potatoes, chopped onion, chopped tomato, chopped cilantro, chopped green chili, salt, red chili powder, cumin powder, coriander powder, and chaat masala.

4. Stir in the lemon juice and mix until well combined.

5. Serve the aloo kabli immediately, garnished with additional chopped cilantro and a squeeze of lemon juice, if desired.

CHURMUR (CRUNCHY FUCHKA SNACK)

Ingredients:

- 1 cup all-purpose flour
- 1/2 cup semolina
- 1 tsp salt
- 1 tsp sugar
- 1 tbsp vegetable oil
- Water, as needed
- Vegetable oil for deep-frying
- 1 cup boiled and mashed potatoes
- 1/2 cup chickpeas, boiled
- 1 small onion, finely chopped
- 2 tbsp chopped cilantro
- 1 tsp red chili powder
- 1 tsp chaat masala
- 1 tsp roasted cumin powder
- 1 tsp tamarind chutney
- 1 tsp green mint chutney
- Lemon juice, to taste

Instructions:

1. In a large mixing bowl, mix together the all-purpose flour, semolina, salt, sugar, vegetable oil, and water to form a soft dough.

2. Cover the dough and let rest for 15-20 minutes.

3. Divide the dough into small balls and roll each ball into a thin circle.

4. Heat the vegetable oil for deep-frying in a large pot over medium heat.

5. Fry the rolled dough circles in the hot oil until puffed and golden brown, about 1-2 minutes on each side.

6. Remove the fried dough circles and let cool slightly.

7. Using your hands, crumble the fried dough circles into small pieces and place in a large mixing bowl.

8. Add the boiled and mashed potatoes, boiled chickpeas, chopped onion, chopped cilantro, red chili powder, chaat masala, roasted cumin powder, tamarind chutney, green mint chutney, and lemon juice to the mixing bowl and mix until well combined.

9. Serve the churmur immediately, garnished with additional chopped cilantro and a squeeze of lemon juice, if desired.

KALA CHANA CHAAT
(BLACK CHICKPEA SALAD)

Ingredients:

- 1 cup dried black chickpeas, soaked overnight
- 1 small onion, chopped
- 1 large tomato, chopped

- 2 tbsp chopped cilantro
- 1 green chili, chopped
- 1 tsp salt
- 1 tsp red chili powder
- 1 tsp cumin powder
- 1 tsp coriander powder
- 1 tsp chaat masala
- 1 tbsp lemon juice

Instructions:

1. Boil the soaked black chickpeas in a large pot of water until tender, about 25-30 minutes.

2. Drain the boiled chickpeas and set aside to cool slightly.

3. In a large mixing bowl, mix together the cooked chickpeas, chopped onion, chopped tomato, chopped cilantro, chopped green chili, salt, red chili powder, cumin powder, coriander powder, and chaat masala.

4. Stir in the lemon juice and mix until well combined.

5. Serve the kala chana chaat immediately, garnished with additional chopped cilantro and a squeeze of lemon juice, if desired.

DESSERTS & SWEETS

ROSHOGOLLA
(SWEET CHEESE BALLS IN SYRUP)

Ingredients:

- 2 liters full-fat milk
- 1/2 cup lemon juice
- 1 cup sugar
- 2 cups water
- 1 tsp cardamom powder
- 1 tbsp rose water (optional)

Instructions:

1. In a large saucepan, bring the milk to a boil over medium heat. Reduce the heat to low and add the lemon juice, stirring constantly.

2. The milk will begin to curdle and the curds will separate from the whey. Use a slotted spoon to transfer the curds to a cheesecloth-lined colander to drain.

3. Tie the corners of the cheesecloth together to form a bundle and hang the bundle over a sink or bowl for 30 minutes to 1 hour, or until all the whey has drained out and the cheese has cooled to room temperature.

4. Knead the cheese in the cheesecloth until it is smooth and pliable. Divide the cheese into 8-10 equal-sized balls.

5. In a large saucepan, combine the sugar and water and bring to a boil over medium heat. Reduce the heat to low and add the cheese balls to the syrup. Simmer the syrup for 10-15 minutes, or until the cheese balls have doubled in size and are heated through.

6. Remove the saucepan from the heat and let the cheese balls cool in the syrup for 30 minutes to 1 hour, or until they have set and the syrup has thickened.

7. Stir in the cardamom powder and rose water, if using.

8. Serve the roshogolla warm or at room temperature, garnished with additional cardamom powder and rose water, if desired.

SANDESH (MILK-BASED SWEET)

Ingredients:

- 2 liters full-fat milk
- 1/2 cup lemon juice
- 1 cup sugar
- 1 tsp cardamom powder
- 1 tbsp rose water (optional)
- Pistachios for garnish (optional)

Instructions:

1. In a large saucepan, bring the milk to a boil over medium heat. Reduce the heat to low and add the lemon juice, stirring constantly.

2. The milk will begin to curdle and the curds will separate from the whey. Use a slotted spoon to transfer the curds to a cheesecloth-lined colander to drain.

3. Tie the corners of the cheesecloth together to form a bundle and hang the bundle over a sink or bowl for 30 minutes to 1 hour, or until all the whey has drained out and the cheese has cooled to room temperature.

4. In a large saucepan, combine the sugar and 1 cup of water and bring to a boil over medium heat. Reduce the heat to low and add the cheese to the syrup. Stir constantly until the sugar has dissolved and the mixture has thickened, about 10-15 minutes.

5. Remove the saucepan from the heat and stir in the cardamom powder and rose water, if using.

6. Pour the mixture into a greased 9x9 inch (23x23 cm) baking dish and let it cool completely to room temperature.

7. Once cooled, cut the sandesh into desired shapes and garnish with chopped pistachios, if desired.

8. Serve the sandesh at room temperature or chilled, garnished with additional cardamom powder and rose water, if desired.

CHOMCHOM (SWEET MILK DESSERT)

Ingredients:

- 2 liters full-fat milk
- 1/2 cup lemon juice
- 1 cup sugar
- 2 cups water
- 1 tsp cardamom powder
- 1 tbsp rose water (optional)
- Pistachios for garnish (optional)

Instructions:

1. In a large saucepan, bring the milk to a boil over medium heat. Reduce the heat to low and add the lemon juice, stirring constantly.

2. The milk will begin to curdle and the curds will separate from the whey. Use a slotted spoon to transfer the curds to a cheesecloth-lined colander to drain.

3. Tie the corners of the cheesecloth together to form a bundle and hang the bundle over a sink or bowl for 30 minutes to 1 hour, or until all the whey has drained out and the cheese has cooled to room temperature.

4. Knead the cheese in the cheesecloth until it is smooth and pliable. Divide the cheese into 8-10 equal-sized balls and shape into oval or cylindrical shapes.

5. In a large saucepan, combine the sugar and water and bring to a boil over medium heat. Reduce the heat to low and add the cheese balls to the syrup. Simmer the syrup for 10-15 minutes, or until the cheese balls have doubled in size and are heated through.

6. Remove the saucepan from the heat and let the cheese balls cool in the syrup for 30 minutes to 1 hour, or until they have set and the syrup has thickened.

7. Stir in the cardamom powder and rose water, if using.

8. Serve the chomchom warm or at room temperature, garnished with chopped pistachios, if desired.

KALO JAM (DARK SWEET CHEESE BALLS)

Ingredients:

- 2 liters full-fat milk
- 1/2 cup lemon juice

- 1 cup jaggery or dark brown sugar
- 2 cups water
- 1 tsp cardamom powder
- 1 tbsp rose water (optional)
- Pistachios for garnish (optional)

Instructions:

1. In a large saucepan, bring the milk to a boil over medium heat. Reduce the heat to low and add the lemon juice, stirring constantly.

2. The milk will begin to curdle and the curds will separate from the whey. Use a slotted spoon to transfer the curds to a cheesecloth-lined colander to drain.

3. Tie the corners of the cheesecloth together to form a bundle and hang the bundle over a sink or bowl for 30 minutes to 1 hour, or until all the whey has drained out and the cheese has cooled to room temperature.

4. Knead the cheese in the cheesecloth until it is smooth and pliable. Divide the cheese into 8-10 equal-sized balls and shape into oval or cylindrical shapes.

5. In a large saucepan, combine the jaggery or dark brown sugar and water and bring to a boil over medium heat. Reduce the heat to low and add the cheese balls to the syrup. Simmer the syrup for 10-15 minutes, or until the cheese balls have doubled in size and are heated through.

6. Remove the saucepan from the heat and let the cheese balls cool in the syrup for 30 minutes to 1 hour, or until they have set and the syrup has thickened.

7. Stir in the cardamom powder and rose water, if using.

8. Serve the kalo jam warm or at room temperature, garnished with chopped pistachios, if desired.

MISHTI DOI (SWEET YOGURT)

Ingredients:

- 2 liters full-fat milk
- 1/2 cup sugar
- 1 tsp cardamom powder
- 1 tbsp rose water (optional)

Instructions:

1. In a large saucepan, bring the milk to a boil over medium heat. Reduce the heat to low and add the sugar, stirring constantly until it has dissolved.

2. Simmer the milk for 1-2 hours, or until it has thickened and reduced to about half its original volume.

3. Remove the saucepan from the heat and stir in the cardamom powder and rose water, if using.4. Pour the mixture into individual serving bowls or a large container and let it cool to room temperature.

5. Cover the bowls or container with plastic wrap and refrigerate for at least 6 hours, or until the mixture has set into a yogurt-like consistency.

6. Serve the mishti doi chilled, garnished with additional cardamom powder and rose water, if desired.

SHEMAI (VERMICELLI DESSERT)

Ingredients:

- 1 cup fine vermicelli noodles
- 2 liters full-fat milk
- 1 cup sugar

- 1 tsp cardamom powder
- 1 tbsp rose water (optional)
- Pistachios for garnish (optional)

Instructions:

1. In a large saucepan, bring the milk to a boil over medium heat. Reduce the heat to low and add the vermicelli noodles, stirring constantly until they have softened, about 5 minutes.

2. Add the sugar to the saucepan and continue to stir until it has dissolved. Simmer the mixture for 1-2 hours, or until it has thickened and reduced to about half its original volume.

3. Remove the saucepan from the heat and stir in the cardamom powder and rose water, if using.

4. Pour the mixture into individual serving bowls or a large container and let it cool to room temperature.

5. Cover the bowls or container with plastic wrap and refrigerate for at least 6 hours, or until the mixture has set into a pudding-like consistency.

6. Serve the shemai chilled, garnished with chopped pistachios, if desired.

FIRNI (RICE PUDDING)

Ingredients:

- 1 cup basmati rice
- 2 liters full-fat milk
- 1 cup sugar
- 1 tsp cardamom powder
- 1 tbsp rose water (optional)
- Pistachios for garnish (optional)

Instructions:

1. Rinse the rice in cold water and drain well.

2. In a large saucepan, bring the milk to a boil over medium heat. Reduce the heat to low and add the rice, stirring constantly.

3. Add the sugar to the saucepan and continue to stir until it has dissolved. Simmer the mixture for 1-2 hours, or until the rice is tender and the mixture has thickened to a pudding-like consistency.

4. Remove the saucepan from the heat and stir in the cardamom powder and rose water, if using.

5. Pour the mixture into individual serving bowls or a large container and let it cool to room temperature.

6. Cover the bowls or container with plastic wrap and refrigerate for at least 6 hours, or until the mixture has set into a pudding-like consistency.

7. Serve the firni chilled, garnished with chopped pistachios, if desired.

PAYESH (RICE AND MILK PUDDING)

Ingredients:

- 1 cup basmati rice
- 2 liters full-fat milk
- 1 cup sugar
- 1 tsp cardamom powder
- 1 tbsp rose water (optional)
- Pistachios for garnish (optional)

Instructions:

1. Rinse the rice in cold water and drain well.

2. In a large saucepan, bring the milk to a boil over medium heat. Reduce the heat to low and add the rice, stirring constantly.

3. Add the sugar to the saucepan and continue to stir until it has dissolved. Simmer the mixture for 1-2 hours, or until the rice is tender and the mixture has thickened to a pudding-like consistency.

4. Remove the saucepan from the heat and stir in the cardamom powder and rose water, if using.

5. Pour the mixture into individual serving bowls or a large container and let it cool to room temperature.

6. Cover the bowls or container with plastic wrap and refrigerate for at least 6 hours, or until the mixture has set into a pudding-like consistency.

7. Serve the payesh chilled, garnished with chopped pistachios, if desired.

KHEER (MILK AND RICE DESSERT)

Ingredients:

- 1 cup basmati rice
- 2 liters full-fat milk
- 1 cup sugar
- 1 tsp cardamom powder
- 1 tbsp rose water (optional)
- Pistachios for garnish (optional)

Instructions:

1. Rinse the rice in cold water and drain well.

2. In a large saucepan, bring the milk to a boil over medium heat. Reduce the heat to low and add the rice, stirring constantly.

3. Add the sugar to the saucepan and continue to stir until it has dissolved. Simmer the mixture for 1-2 hours, or until the rice is tender and the mixture has thickened to a pudding-like consistency.

4. Remove the saucepan from the heat and stir in the cardamom powder and rose water, if using.

5. Pour the mixture into individual serving bowls or a large container and let it cool to room temperature.

6. Cover the bowls or container with plastic wrap and refrigerate for at least 6 hours, or until the mixture has set into a pudding-like consistency.

7. Serve the kheer chilled, garnished with chopped pistachios, if desired.

NARKEL NARU (COCONUT BALLS)

Ingredients:

- 1 cup unsweetened shredded coconut
- 1 cup sugar
- 1 cup milk
- 1 tsp cardamom powder
- Pinch of saffron (optional)

Instructions:

1. In a large saucepan, combine the coconut, sugar, and milk. Cook over medium heat, stirring constantly, until the mixture comes to a boil.

2. Reduce the heat to low and continue to cook the mixture, stirring constantly, until it has thickened and the sugar has dissolved, about 10-15 minutes.

3. Remove the saucepan from the heat and stir in the cardamom powder and saffron, if using.

4. Let the mixture cool to room temperature.

5. Using a spoon or your hands, form the mixture into small balls.

6. Place the balls on a sheet of parchment paper and let them cool completely.

7. Serve the narkel naru at room temperature or chilled.

RASMALAI (SWEET CHEESE DUMPLINGS)

Ingredients:

- **For the cheese dumplings:**

    - 1 cup paneer (cottage cheese)
    - 1 cup all-purpose flour
    - 1 tsp sugar
    - 1 tsp baking powder
    - 1/4 tsp baking soda
    - 1/4 tsp salt
    - 1/4 cup water

- **For the syrup:**

- 2 liters full-fat milk
- 1 cup sugar
- 1 tsp cardamom powder
- 1 tbsp rose water (optional)

Instructions:

1. To make the cheese dumplings: In a large bowl, crumble the paneer. Add the flour, sugar, baking powder , baking soda, and salt and mix until well combined. Add the water a little at a time, mixing until a dough forms.

2. Roll the dough into small balls, about the size of a golf ball. Place the balls on a plate and set aside.

3. To make the syrup: In a large saucepan, bring the milk to a boil over medium heat. Reduce the heat to low and add the sugar, stirring until it has dissolved. Simmer the mixture for 1-2 hours, or until it has thickened to a syrup-like consistency.

4. Add the cardamom powder and rose water, if using, to the syrup and stir to combine.

5. In a separate large saucepan, bring a large pot of water to a boil. Gently drop the cheese balls into the boiling water and cook for 2-3 minutes, or until they have puffed up slightly.

6. Remove the cheese balls from the water with a slotted spoon and place them in the syrup. Let them soak for 10-15 minutes, or until they have absorbed the syrup.

7. Serve the rasmalai chilled, garnished with chopped pistachios or almonds, if desired.

CHANAR JILAPI (SWEET CHEESE SPIRALS)

Ingredients:

- 1 cup all-purpose flour
- 1 cup paneer (cottage cheese), crumbled
- 1/2 cup sugar
- 1 tsp cardamom powder
- 1/2 tsp baking powder
- 1/4 tsp baking soda
- 1/4 tsp salt
- 1/4 cup water
- Vegetable oil for frying

Instructions:

1. In a large bowl, combine the flour, crumbled paneer, sugar, cardamom powder, baking powder, baking soda, and salt.

2. Add the water a little at a time, mixing until a dough forms.

3. Divide the dough into small balls, about the size of a golf ball.

4. Roll each ball into a long, thin rope, about 1/4 inch thick and 12 inches long.

5. Twist the rope into a spiral shape and press the ends together to secure the shape.

6. In a large saucepan, heat the oil over medium heat. Gently place the cheese spirals in the hot oil and fry, turning occasionally, until they are golden brown and crispy, about 2-3 minutes.

7. Remove the cheese spirals from the oil with a slotted spoon and place them on a paper towel-lined plate to drain any excess oil.

8. Serve the chanar jilapi warm or at room temperature.

PANTUA (FRIED SWEET BALLS)

Ingredients:

- 1 cup all-purpose flour
- 1 cup semolina
- 1/2 cup sugar
- 1 tsp baking powder
- 1/4 tsp baking soda
- 1/4 tsp salt
- 1/2 cup yogurt
- 1/4 cup water
- Vegetable oil for frying

Instructions:

1. In a large bowl, combine the flour, semolina, sugar, baking powder, baking soda, and salt.

2. Add the yogurt and water and mix until a dough forms.

3. Divide the dough into small balls, about the size of a golf ball.

4. In a large saucepan, heat the oil over medium heat. Gently place the dough balls in the hot oil and fry, turning occasionally, until they are golden brown and crispy, about 2-3 minutes.

5. Remove the pantua from the oil with a slotted spoon and place them on a paper towel-lined plate to drain any excess oil.

6. Serve the pantua warm or at room temperature.

LADDU (SWEET ROUND BALLS)

Ingredients:

- 1 cup semolina
- 1 cup sugar
- 1 cup ghee
- 1 tsp cardamom powder
- 1/2 cup chopped nuts (such as almonds or cashews), optional

Instructions:

1. In a large saucepan, combine the semolina, sugar, and ghee. Cook over medium heat, stirring constantly, until the mixture turns golden brown and fragrant, about 10-15 minutes.

2. Remove the saucepan from the heat and stir in the cardamom powder and chopped nuts, if using.

3. Let the mixture cool for a few minutes, until it is cool enough to handle.

4. Using your hands, form the mixture into small balls.

5. Place the balls on a sheet of parchment paper and let them cool completely.

6. Serve the laddu at room temperature or chilled.

MALPUA (SWEET PANCAKES)

Ingredients:

- 1 cup all-purpose flour
- 1/2 cup semolina
- 1/2 cup sugar

- 1 tsp cardamom powder
- 1 tsp baking powder
- 1/4 tsp baking soda
- 1/4 tsp salt
- 1/2 cup yogurt
- 1/4 cup water
- Vegetable oil for frying

Instructions:

1. In a large bowl, combine the flour, semolina, sugar, cardamom powder, baking powder, baking soda, and salt.

2. Add the yogurt and water and mix until a batter forms.

3. In a large saucepan, heat a small amount of oil over medium heat. Pour about 1/4 cup of the batter into the hot oil and spread it into a thin, circular shape.

4. Fry the malpua until it is golden brown on both sides, about 2-3 minutes per side.

5. Repeat with the remaining batter, adding more oil as needed.

6. Serve the malpua warm or at room temperature, topped with syrup or honey, if desired.

GURER PAYESH (JAGGERY RICE PUDDING)

Ingredients:

- 1 cup basmati rice
- 2 cups water
- 2 cups milk
- 1 cup jaggery

- 1 tsp cardamom powder
- 1 tsp vanilla extract
- 1/2 cup raisins
- 1/2 cup chopped nuts (such as almonds or cashews), optional

Instructions:

1. Rinse the rice in cold water and drain well.

2. In a large saucepan, bring the water to a boil over high heat. Add the rice and stir to combine.

3. Reduce the heat to low, cover the saucepan, and let the rice simmer for 15-20 minutes, or until it is fully cooked and the water has been absorbed.

4. In a separate saucepan, bring the milk to a boil over medium heat. Reduce the heat to low and add the jaggery, stirring until it has dissolved.

5. Stir in the cardamom powder, vanilla extract, raisins, and chopped nuts, if using.

6. Add the cooked rice to the milk mixture and stir to combine.

7. Cook the gurer payesh over low heat, stirring constantly, until it has thickened to a pudding-like consistency, about 10-15 minutes.

8. Serve the gurer payesh warm or chilled, topped with additional chopped nuts or raisins, if desired.

PITHA (RICE CAKE)

Ingredients:

- 1 cup rice flour
- 1/2 cup water
- 1/2 cup milk
- 1/2 cup sugar
- 1 tsp cardamom powder
- 1/4 tsp salt
- Vegetable oil for frying

Instructions:

1. In a large bowl, mix together the rice flour, water, milk, sugar, cardamom powder, and salt until a batter forms.

2. In a large saucepan, heat a small amount of oil over medium heat. Pour about 1/4 cup of the batter into the hot oil and spread it into a thin, circular shape.

3. Fry the pitha until it is golden brown on both sides, about 2-3 minutes per side.

4. Repeat with the remaining batter, adding more oil as needed.

5. Serve the pitha warm or at room temperature, topped with syrup or honey, if desired.

RECIPES LIST

BREAKFAST
CHIRE BHAJA (FRIED FLATTENED RICE) 5
RADHABALLABHI (STUFFED DEEP-FRIED BREAD) 6
MUGHLAI PARATHA (STUFFED AND FRIED BREAD) 8
ALUR DOM (SPICY POTATO CURRY) 9
DIMER JHOL (EGG CURRY) 11

APPETIZERS & SNACKS
SINGARA (SAMOSA) 13
PIYAJU (LENTIL FRITTERS) 14
BEGUNI (EGGPLANT FRITTERS) 15
ALOO CHOP (POTATO FRITTERS) 16
CHINGRI PAKORA (SHRIMP FRITTERS) 17
DALER BORA (LENTIL DUMPLINGS) 18
MURI GHONTO (PUFFED RICE SNACK) 19
JHAL MURI (SPICY PUFFED RICE) 20
CHOTPOTI (SPICY CHICKPEA SNACK) 21
FUCHKA (PANIPURI) 22
VEGETABLE CUTLET 23
SHOBJI PITHA (VEGETABLE STUFFED RICE CAKE) ... 24
CHITAI PITHA (THIN RICE CAKE) 25
PATISHAPTA (SWEET RICE CREPES) 26
BHAPA PITHA (STEAMED RICE CAKE) 27
PULI PITHA (SWEET RICE DUMPLINGS) 28

CHUI JHAL MURI (RICE PUFF SNACK) 29

JHURI BHAJA (THIN POTATO CRISPS) 29

RICE DISHES

BHUNA KHICHURI (FRIED RICE AND LENTIL DISH) ...31

MOROG POLAO (CHICKEN AND RICE DISH) 32

KALA BHUNA POLAO (BEEF AND RICE DISH) 33

ILISH POLAO (HILSA FISH AND RICE DISH) 35

SHORSHE BATA ILISH 36

CHINGRI POLAO (SHRIMP AND RICE DISH) 37

MISHTI POLAO (SWEET RICE) 38

KICHURI (RICE AND LENTIL DISH) 39

PANTA BHAT (FERMENTED RICE) 40

KHICHDI (RICE AND LENTIL PORRIDGE) 41

CURRIES AND STEWS

DHANSAAK 43

DAL MAKHANI 44

TARKA DAL 45

CHANA DAL 46

MASOOR DAL 47

BEEF BHUNA 48

CHICKEN KORMA 50

CHICKEN JALFREZI 51

MUTTON REZALA 52

KOSHA MANGSHO (SLOW-COOKED MEAT) 53

CHICKEN BHARTA 54

MURGHI MASALLAM 56

SHOBJI DAL) 57

ECHORER DALNA 58

LAU CHINGRI 59

ALU VORTA (MASHED POTATO) 61

BAINGAN BHARTA (MASHED EGGPLANT) 62

SHUTKI BHORTA (DRIED FISH MASH) 63

SHOBJI BHORTA (MIXED VEGETABLE MASH) 64

BHINDI BHAJI (OKRA STIR-FRY) 65

NIRAMISH (MIXED VEGETABLE CURRY) 66

LABRA (MIXED VEGETABLE STEW) 67

CHORCHORI (MIXED VEGETABLE MEDLEY) 69

PALONG SHAAK (SPINACH CURRY) 70

SHAAK BHAJA (FRIED LEAFY GREENS) 71

CAULIFLOWER AND POTATO CURRY 71

PUMPKIN AND SHRIMP CURRY 73

FISH & SEAFOOD

MAACH BHAJA (FRIED FISH) 75

DOI MAACH (FISH IN YOGURT SAUCE) 76

RUI MAACHER JHOL (FISH CURRY) 77

ILISH BHAJA (FRIED HILSA FISH) 78

SHORSHE ILISH (HILSA FISH IN MUSTARD SAUCE) ... 78

PABDA MACHER JHAL (PABDA FISH CURRY) 79

CHITAL MACHER MUITHA (FISH DUMPLINGS) 81

KOI MACHER JHOL...82

SHRIMP MALAI CURRY 83

CHINGRI MACHER MALAIKARI 84

CHINGRI BHAPE (STEAMED SHRIMP).............................85

LOITTA MACHER JHURI...86

CRAB KALIA (CRAB CURRY)..87

TILAPIA SHORSHE 88

RUPCHANDA MACHER JHOL...89

MEATS

CHICKEN ROAST..91

MUTTON KORMA 92

BEEF KALA BHUNA...93

CHICKEN CHAAP 94

DUCK CURRY..95

QUAIL CURRY 96

BEEF TEHARI..97

BREADS

LUCHI (DEEP-FRIED BREAD)..99

PARATHA (LAYERED FLATBREAD) 100

NAAN (LEAVENED BREAD)...101

KULCHA (LEAVENED BREAD WITH STUFFING) 102

ROTI (UNLEAVENED BREAD)...103

TANDOORI ROTI (CLAY OVEN-BAKED BREAD).........104

CHAPATI (THIN UNLEAVENED BREAD).......................105

TAFTAN (LEAVENED BREAD WITH SAFFRON) 106
PURI (DEEP-FRIED PUFFED BREAD) 107
BAKARKHANI (SWEET FLAKY BREAD) 108
SHEERMAL (SWEET SAFFRON-FLAVORED BREAD) .. 109

BEVERAGES
BORHANI (SPICED YOGURT DRINK) 111
LASSI (YOGURT-BASED DRINK) 112
CHAAS (SPICED BUTTERMILK) 112
GHOL (SWEET YOGURT DRINK) 113
AAM PANNA (RAW MANGO DRINK) 113
LEBUR SHARBAT (LEMONADE) 114
TAMARIND SHARBAT (TAMARIND DRINK) 115
FALOODA (MILK, ROSE SYRUP DESSERT DRINK) 115
DUDH SHORBOT (MILK, ROSE SYRUP DRINK) 116

PICKLES & CHUTNEYS
AAM ACHAR (MANGO PICKLE) 117
MIXED VEGETABLE ACHAR 118
LIME PICKLE 119
TOMATO CHUTNEY 120
GREEN MANGO CHUTNEY 121
TAMARIND CHUTNEY 122
CORIANDER CHUTNEY 123
MINT CHUTNEY 123

SALADS

KACHUMBER SALAD 125
CUCUMBER RAITA 125
TOMATO AND ONION SALAD 126
CHICKPEA SALAD 126

SOUPS

MULLIGATAWNY SOUP 128
LENTIL SOUP 129
VEGETABLE SOUP 130
CHICKEN SOUP 131
MUTTON SOUP 132
FISH SOUP 133
SHRIMP SOUP 134

SIDES

PAPADUM (CRISPY LENTIL WAFERS) 136
BHORTA (MASHED VEGETABLES) 137
RAITA (YOGURT-BASED SIDE DISH) 138
FRIED PLANTAINS 139
BRINJAL FRY (EGGPLANT FRY) 139

STREET FOOD

JHAL MURI (SPICY PUFFED RICE) 141
FUCHKA (PANIPURI) 142

GHUGNI (SPICY YELLOW PEAS).................................. 143
ALOO KABLI (SPICY POTATO SALAD)......................... 144
CHURMUR (CRUNCHY FUCHKA SNACK) 145
KALA CHANA CHAAT (BLACK CHICKPEA SALAD) 146

Made in the USA
Columbia, SC
12 May 2023